Sensing the Seasons

Learning Centers for the Church Year

PHYLLIS VOS WEZEMAN & ANNA L. LIECHTY

✳ The Pastoral Center

Dedication

To Tina Kaser Morales ...

... who baked so many apple-cinnamon ornaments
to scent the church for the very first "Sense the Season." A.L.L.

To Jacob William Elsbury ...

... may every season of your life be a celebration. P.V.W.

Thanks

To Judith Harris Chase ...

... who inspired this project.

ISBN 978-1-949628-25-8
Printed in the United States of America.
10 9 8 7 6 5 4 3 2   23 22 21 20

Copyright © 2020 Phyllis Vos Wezeman and Anna L. Liechty. All rights reserved. Published by The Pastoral Center / PastoralCenter.com. You are allowed to share and make unlimited copies of this document for use within the parish or school community that licensed it. If you serve more than one community, each should purchase its own license. You may not post this document to any web site (without explicit permission to do so). Thank you for cooperating with our honor system regarding our eResource licenses.

The Scripture passages contained herein are from the *New Revised Standard Version of the Bible*, copyright © 1989, by the Division of Christian Education of the National Council of Churches in the U.S.A. All rights reserved.

Image of hot cross buns by jules, originally posted to Flickr as hot cross buns - fig & pecan, CC BY 2.0, https://commons.wikimedia.org/w/index.php?curid=10391073.

Sense icon images copyright 2020 Twitter, Inc and other contributors. Graphics licensed under CC-BY 4.0: https://creativecommons.org/licenses/by/4.0/.

Table of Contents

Foreword _____ 5
The Church Year _____ 7
The Five Senses _____ 9
Learning Centers _____ 11

Sensing the Church Year 15
Clock Face Calendars _____ 16
Colorful Weavings _____ 19
Bottle Scale Songs _____ 21
Snack Sacks _____ 24
Beaded Pins _____ 28

Sensing Advent 33
Decorated Candles _____ 34
Lavender Sachets _____ 35
Music Mobiles _____ 36
Cookie Gifts _____ 37
Mini Wreaths _____ 39

Sensing Christmas 41
Stained Glass Ornaments _____ 42
Pomander Balls _____ 43
Mini Jingle Bell Wreaths _____ 44
Gingerbread with Toppings _____ 45
Evergreen Prints _____ 46

Sensing Epiphany 47
Sand Painted Cards _____ 48
Incense Holders _____ 49
Sound Effects _____ 50
Crisp Rice Star Treats _____ 51
Shell Covered Chests _____ 52

Sensing Lent 53
Cross Symbols _____ 54
Scented Soap Balls _____ 58
Prayer Poems _____ 59
Lenten Foods Concentration Game ____ 62
Educational Eggs _____ 68

Sensing Easter 71
Butterfly Banners _____ 72
Egg Decorations _____ 74
Flower Pot Bells _____ 75
Butterfly Shaped Snacks _____ 76
Block Print Cards _____ 77

Sensing Pentecost 79
Trinity Triptych _____ 80
Guided Meditation _____ 82
Bottle Puppets _____ 85
Meringues _____ 86
Dove Mobiles _____ 88

Sensing Ordinary Time 91
Wire Fish Pendants _____ 92
Herb Bottles and Gardens _____ 93
Rhythm Instruments _____ 96
Memorizing Bible Verses _____ 98
Flowering Branches _____ 99

Resources 101
Age Group Suggestions _____ 103
Catholic Church Year Overview _____ 105
Ecumenical Church Year Overview ___ 107
Church Year Themes _____ 109
Methods Index _____ 111
Scripture Index _____ 114
About the Authors _____ 116

Foreword

It was the last day of my third trip to Russia. On trip one, I led a six-week international youth exchange program in Russia and the Ukraine. Trips two and three were to conduct classes on "Methods of Teaching" at the St. Petersburg State University of Pedagogical Art. At the final meeting of trip three—also known as the evaluation session—the administrators invited me to be faculty for their upcoming international conference: "The Bible as a Historic, Cultural Document." Besides the university, the event would be co-sponsored by the Mayor's Office on Education and the Russian Orthodox Church. My hosts asked me to come back and present four days of classes on methods of teaching Bible stories.

Once home, I began pondering, praying, and panicking. It was July and the event was in November. As I sat at my computer one morning, I uttered an urgent plea for God's help. "Dear God, if you really want me to do this, please give me a plan—now—so I can work the plan—soon!" With that, I picked up a pen and began to doodle letters and words on a piece of paper. For some reason, I kept writing four letters over and over again—L-O-V-E. That's it, I gasped, as I offered "thanks" to the source of my inspiration. The entire message of the Bible could be summarized in one word—L-O-V-E. And, what better way to teach the story of God's love than to use a plan that was already in place—the structure of the church calendar.

Since I wanted to start at the beginning of the stories in the Bible—with the account of Adam and Eve in the book of Genesis—I associated the season of Advent, our time of preparing for God's gift of the Savior, with the first letter of the word "LOVE"—the "L." Class One would consider the "Lessons" of Old Testament "Lives" and share God's plan to send the Messiah. Day Two would cover the seasons of Christmas and Epiphany and emphasize that God's "Only" son became "Our" Savior. With Lent and Easter combined on Day Three, the "V" for "Victor" would stress that Jesus, the Savior, conquered sin and death so that we might have the "Victory" of eternal life. Class Four, the season of Pentecost, would summarize the message that God's "L-O-V-E" is for "Everyone"—"Everywhere." It seemed so simple, but it said it all—a four letter summary of the entire Bible.

At the last session, an elderly man who had been in the course for the four days remarked: "We heard many speakers this week who presented information that filled our heads, but what you shared also touched our hearts. We'll always remember that the message of the Bible is simply about God's 'L-O-V-E.'"

As you use the activities in this book, and share them with the participants at learning centers, my prayer is that lessons will be learned and lives will be touched by the simple, and significant, message of God's L-O-V-E.

—Phyllis Vos Wezeman

Introduction

Sensing the Seasons: Learning Centers for the Church Year is a book of activities that connects the five senses with the significant stories of Advent, Christmas, Epiphany, Lent, Easter, Pentecost, and Ordinary Time. Used in liturgical, educational, and home settings, materials in this resource will help children, youth, and adults explore and experience their faith, not only during these important times, but throughout life.

This book, *Sensing the Seasons*, contains eight sections. Each portion reviews a period of the liturgical cycle through five learning centers. Each learning center offers an activity to examine the important day or season through the five senses—sight, smell, sound, taste, and touch. All eight themed units begin with a brief summary of the day or season.

The Church Year

When using the theme of the church year, research information on your specific faith community's celebrations of seasons and feasts. For example:

- Ask your pastor or parish priest if they prefer the term church/liturgical calendar, cycle, or year.
- Consult the altar guild, sacristan, or the liturgy/worship committee about colors:
  - using green, gold, or white for Epiphany
  - using black, red, or purple on Good Friday
- Find out from the choir director or the church secretary if the bulletin refers to a season of Epiphany, Ordinary Time, or Sunday after Epiphany
- Inquire of the religious education teacher or the youth leader if the curriculum uses feast day, holy day, or time period.
- Poll the elementary school learner or the middle school student to find out if the correct word is day, festival, or season.
- Question the parent or the long-time member if Ordinary Time, Growing Time, or Kingdomtide is used after Pentecost Sunday.

Most likely, there will be differences of opinions—even within the same congregation, the same diocese or synod, and the same denomination or faith tradition. Even online articles and printed books, denominational documents, Facebook pages, monthly newsletters, social media posts, and weekly bulletins offer contradictory information about vocabulary, start/end dates, colors, and more related to the Christian calendar. Yet, even though there are differences there are many things on which everyone agrees.

First, and foremost, people concur that the church calendar is a pattern that helps Christians remember—and live—the entire story of salvation each year. In the Old Testament, Exodus 13:1-10, God instructs Moses to lead Israel to schedule regular and repeated observances that will keep God's mighty acts always in mind for generations to come. By doing this, the faith of all ages—throughout time—will be centered in God's savings acts in history. Deuteronomy 6:1-9 says it well:

> *Now this is the commandment—the statutes and the ordinances—that the Lord your God charged me to teach you to observe in the land that you are about to cross into and occupy, so that you and your children and your children's children, may fear the Lord your God all the days of your life, and keep all his decrees and his commandments that I am commanding you, so that your days may be long. Hear therefore, O Israel, and observe them diligently, so that it may go well with you, and so that you may multiply greatly in a land flowing with milk and honey, as the Lord, the God of your ancestors, has promised you. Hear, O Israel: The Lord is our God, the Lord alone. You shall love the Lord your God with all your heart, and with all your soul, and with all your might. Keep these words that I am commanding you today in your heart. Recite them to your children and talk about them when you are at home and when you are away, when you lie down and when you rise. Bind them as a sign on your hand, fix them as an emblem on your forehead, and write them on the doorposts of your house and on your gates.*

In the New Testament, 1 Timothy 3:15, Paul counsels Timothy, the pastor at Ephesus, that the heart of the church's faith is directly related to remembering God's saving acts in the birth, ministry, and reign of Jesus Christ. Passages in Philippians and Titus remind Christians today of the reason:

Philippians 2:8-11

> *He humbled himself and became obedient to the point of death—even death on a cross. Therefore God also highly exalted him and gave him the name that is above every name, so that at the name of Jesus every knee should bend, in heaven and on earth and under the earth, and every tongue should confess that Jesus Christ is Lord, to the glory of God the Father.*

Titus 2:13-14

> *While we wait for the blessed hope and the manifestation of the glory of our great God and Savior, Jesus Christ. He it is who gave himself for us that he might redeem us from all iniquity and purify for himself a people of his own who are zealous for good deeds.*

In the early church, during the fourth and fifth centuries, leaders suggested that Christians intentionally find a way to keep time that would be a fitting celebration of the Gospel message.

The Christian year always begins with the season of Advent in anticipation of the coming of Christ, celebrates Jesus' birth at Christmas, and his ministry during Epiphany. Throughout Lent, the church remembers Jesus' teachings and prepares for his suffering, observes his death during Holy Week, celebrates Christ's victorious resurrection on Easter, and marks the outpouring of the Holy Spirit at Pentecost. After Pentecost, the church observes a period of Ordinary Time—a way of counting the Sundays and weeks of discipleship and mission until the new year begins again in Advent.

Sensing the Seasons provides interactive designs to help people of all ages explore and experience seven significant periods of the liturgical cycle—Advent, Christmas, Epiphany, Lent, Easter, Pentecost, and Ordinary Time. Language used throughout this book incorporates many terms to help participants become aware of the vocabulary as well as its meaning.

It is important—actually imperative—that those coordinating the learning centers provided in this book take time to determine the pattern of the church year used in their own tradition. After that, the specific information must be incorporated into the activities and lessons used to celebrate the story of salvation in liturgical and educational settings in congregations, homes, and schools.

Since the church year also provides a way of understanding the Christian life—baptism into Christ's death and resurrection (Romans 6), communion with Christ through the Lord's Supper (Luke 22:19-20), and the empowerment to mission through the gift of the Holy Spirit (Acts 2:1-4), the liturgical cycle presents a means of public and personal growth for believers. In addition, it offers a way for Jesus' followers to join their hearts with Christians throughout history and throughout the world.

In the end, while there may be variations in how the Christian year is interpreted and celebrated from one congregation or denomination to the next, the ultimate goal might be summed up in the words of one of the most familiar texts in the Bible, John 3:16:

> *For God so loved the world that he gave his only Son, so that everyone who believes in him may not perish but may have eternal life.*

The Five Senses

In *Sensing the Seasons*, the suggested activities employ all of the senses in order to help participants remember the story, comprehend its meaning, and express the joy of the Gospel message. Suggested approaches through these pages will help participants—children, youth, and adults—experience the message of the days and seasons by relating the abstract ideas behind them to the very real experiences of sight, smell, sound, taste, and touch.

Sensing Advent

The season of Advent surrounds us with sensory possibilities from visual displays of wreaths, to the comforting sounds of carols, the fragrant smell of pine, the sweet taste of cookies, and the smooth surface of ornaments. Using *Sensing the Seasons*' suggestions can expand these opportunities to involve the senses during Advent and can heighten each participants' awareness of the anticipated arrival of Christ on Christmas day.

Sensing Christmas

The twelve days of Christmas already bombard the senses with much to see, hear, smell, taste, and touch. But rather than feeling overwhelmed, participants who have been prepared throughout Advent can be ready to connect Christmas impressions with the sustaining message of faith—ready to share that message in a new year.

Sensing Epiphany

Preparing in Advent and celebrating during Christmas leads logically to sharing the message received through our senses throughout Epiphany. The sights, smells, sounds, textures, and tastes of the journey of faith can make the idea of a Messiah more real. Possibilities for exploration found in *Sensing the Seasons* may be enough to inspire participants to be followers of a star and to be open to God's surprises every step of the way.

Sensing Lent

Lent may seem more abstract and difficult to communicate than other parts of the Christian message. Concepts of sin, repentance, and temptation can be difficult to grasp intellectually, especially for younger disciples. Even though death is a concrete concept, we usually avoid the topic and substitute euphemisms. To be successful in reaching out with the challenging journey of Lent, the church must find ways to make the topics of sacrifice and choices understandable, beginning by acknowledging that authentic learning comes by involving participants actively in experiences that touch the senses.

Sensing Easter

The joy of Easter and new life may seem simple to share at first, but to engage discussion and explore questions about eternal life and the meaning of Jesus' sacrifice can make Easter lessons challenging to present. To move children and youth beyond the Easter bunny and jelly beans to the empty tomb and the risen Savior requires thoughtful and meaningful activities that engage both mind and body. *Sensing the Seasons*' activity centers help engage participants in learning experiences that open hearts and help participants discover a way of life built on the hope found in the risen Christ.

Sensing Pentecost

The Pentecost story can be shared meaningfully using a sensory approach. The wind and fire of the coming of the Spirit give us real ways to understand God's power and warming presence. Use the events and ideas outlined in *Sensing the Seasons* to help everyone see the tongues of flame, smell the fresh wind of the Spirit, hear the good news proclaimed in many languages, sample the tastes found in the busy marketplace, and feel the warmth of the fellowship of faith.

Sensing Ordinary Time

After the powerful, sensory message of Pentecost, the long weeks that follow can seem anticlimactic. This time of learning discipleship, of growing in faith, and of spreading the good news of the Gospel can get lost in the shuffle of summer and fall activities. With the help of *Sensing the Seasons*, this ordinary time can become extra-ordinary, as participants look more deeply, listen more carefully, and become more open to each scent, flavor, and feeling that awakens our hearts to more faithful living.

Learning Centers

What?

A Learning Center may be defined as the focal point of activity for the purpose of acquiring knowledge or skill. It must contain information on a topic and instructions for a task in addition to the equipment and supplies necessary to complete the assignment.

Learning Centers:
- create an opportunity for learning to occur
- develop discovery learning techniques
- emphasize hands-on experiences
- focus attention on specific tasks and topics
- foster cooperative learning
- promote critical thinking skills
- provide self-directed, individualized instruction
- release ideas and imagination.

Learning Centers may supplement an existing curriculum, become an additional or alternative program, or be used as a module during a specific church season or throughout a summer session.

Where?

Learning Centers fit into many settings—educational and liturgical—in churches, homes, and schools.

In liturgical settings, they are ideal for Children's Liturgy of the Word or Children's Church. In addition, they could be set up as worship centers in part of a sanctuary or near an entrance to a gathering space.

In educational contexts, incorporate learning centers into traditional programs of faith formation like general religious education, sacramental preparation, Sunday School, and youth groups. Learning Centers work well for year-round ministries such as before and after school programs, kids' clubs, and mid-week sessions. They are perfect for seasonal offerings at camps, retreats, and vacation Bible school. They may be used during adult education courses, community programs, family nights, intergenerational gatherings, and seasonal events.

Learning Centers are ideal for providing liturgical experiences and educational lessons in homes and schools, too.

Who?

Learning Centers are for all ages—children, youth, and adults. People can participate as graded classes, specific programs, family units, and intergenerational groups. Boys and girls in upper elementary grades, tweens in middle school, and young adults in high school, as well as children and parents, and middle-aged to older adults should be able to function as independent learners, partners, or small groups. Pre-schoolers will need teacher or parental guidance in order to hear the directions and use the materials.

While learning centers should be designed for students to work alone or in small groups, there are many ways to manage the number of people at a given station at the same time. Self-direction is ideal, but sometimes a little structure facilitates transitions between and among the varied opportunities. Some examples are:

- allow students to self-select based on availability.
- set up a specific number of chairs and state that if they are filled others must wait their turn.

- assign participants to a timed rotation.
- hand out "tickets" to learning centers so numbers and choices can be limited in a way that avoids competition over preferred activities.
- use a gong, cymbal, bell, or other auditory signal to announce the time for changing centers or ending an activity. Give students three to five minutes to finish and tidy up from activities before asking them to move to a new location.

Be sure instructions include a way for students to add their names to their projects and know where to put their work until it's ready to display or take home.

When?

Learning Centers may be used for specific classes, an entire semester, or throughout a special day or season of the church calendar. They may fit into a regular session or be offered for an event or festival. There is no limit to the day of the week, the time of the day, or the month of the year.

In home settings activity areas might be arranged from time-to-time or be available on a continuous basis.

How?

Learning Centers may be created in many ways. They can be set up on table tops, desks, and counters or created on bulletin, chalk, or white boards, floors, or walls. In essence, an activity station can be constructed on any surface that will hold the essential elements to achieve the desired goals. Learning Centers may be extremely efficient, containing the bare essentials required for achieving the desired results or extraordinarily elaborate with bountiful enhancements to supplement the anticipated outcomes.

Learning Centers for each of the five senses—sight, smell, sound, taste, and touch—in the eight segments of *Sensing the Seasons*—the church year, Advent, Christmas, Epiphany, Lent, Easter, Pentecost, and Ordinary Time—are provided in an easy-to-use four-part format.

Activity

Names the activity or project for the specific station.

Materials

Offers an alphabetical list, in check off format, of equipment and supplies needed for the center. Most of the materials will be items on-hand such as glue, markers, pencils or pens, scissors, and tape. It is important to note, however, that in several cases unique supplies will have to be gathered or unusual materials may need to be purchased.

Advance Preparation

Lists activities that must be done before the participants arrive for the session. If resource sheets need to be copied or printed for the center it is noted here.

Directions on gathering on-hand supplies, adjusting and duplicating instructions to place in the center, and setting up the actual activity area are not noted in advance preparation.

Method

Provides complete, step-by-step, instructions for accomplishing the task. Of course, if there are variations to the activity or adaptations to the interpretation of the church year the directions must be adjusted before they are copied and posted.

Each of the eight chapters of *Sensing the Seasons* begins with an overview of the specific period of the church calendar.

If possible, gather the group that will participate in the Learning Center projects before they start at the specific stations. Use a format such as:

Gather

- Begin by playing a game or singing a song as participants arrive.
- Convene the group by offering a prayer, telling a Bible story, and singing a song.
- Provide an overview of the centers and offer specific directions for each site.

Explore

- Provide time for participants to engage in each center—individually, in pairs, in small groups, or with a guide in the case of young learners.

Celebrate

- Take time to share experiences and projects.
- Close with song and prayer.
- Enjoy refreshments.

Why?

Activities in self-directed learning centers offer the opportunity for participants to grow in at least eight areas. These include:

- **Intellectual**: Participants strengthen their reading, writing, and problem-solving skills, learn the use of new materials, and enhance their knowledge of biblical stories and scriptural themes.
- **Physical**: Pupils develop gross and fine motor skills as well as hand-eye coordination.
- **Social**: Students gain a sense of responsibility and learn cooperation as they interact with others.
- **Emotional**: People learn to express their feelings through involvement in individual and group activities.
- **Perceptual**: Learners explore the use of color and shape and foster greater skill in working in various media.
- **Creative**: Participants expand their imagination and learn diversity in the use of materials while completing projects.
- **Aesthetic**: Children, youth, and adults experience teaching methods such as art, banners/textiles, creative writing, culinary, games, music, puppetry, and storytelling as art.
- **Spiritual**: Disciples grow in an understanding of and an appreciation for God's gifts to each person and to the world.

Sensing the Church Year

Psalm 22:27-31

> *All the ends of the earth shall remember and turn to the Lord; and all the families of the nations shall worship before him. For dominion belongs to the Lord, and he rules over the nations. To him, indeed, shall all who sleep in the earth bow down; before him shall bow all who go down to the dust, and I shall live for him. Posterity will serve him; future generations will be told about the Lord, and proclaim his deliverance to a people yet unborn, saying that he has done it.*

Calendars help to provide the structure for all aspects of our lives, and the church is no exception. Just like the secular calendar reminds us of Valentine hearts or Thanksgiving turkeys, the church calendar invites us to explore the story of salvation as we experience the festivals of faith. The church year coordinates the message of seven basic days and seasons—Advent, Christmas, Epiphany, Lent, Easter, Pentecost, and Ordinary Time—with slight variations among the denominations. Throughout this cycle, we experience the life and ministry of Jesus and the empowering of his church to carry on the work God began in creation. Those stories become part of the rhythm of our lives—anticipated, celebrated, savored, and shared by all God's people. Rather than treasured fragments of disconnected text, the Bible becomes the woven fabric of a seamless garment, with each season flowing meaningfully to the next, completing the cycle, yet leading us to begin again the wonderful journey of faithful discipleship.

To understand the focus and the flavor of the church year, five learning centers—sight, smell, sound, taste, and touch—provide an overview of the liturgical cycle.

Note that the Resources section at the end of this book contains general handouts on the structure of the church year that can be particularly helpful with this chapter.

SENSING THE CHURCH YEAR

Clock Face Calendars

Materials

- Awl or compass point
- Cardboard rounds from cake or pizza
- Copy machine or printer
- Crayons, markers, or colored pencils
- Glue
- Paper for copy machine or printer
- Paper fasteners, brass brads (1"- 1½" long)
- Pencils
- Poster board, black
- Resource sheets:
  - Chart for Church Year
  - Pattern for Church Year Clock
  - The Church Year Overview sheets in the Resources section could also be helpful.
- Scissors

Advance Preparation

- Duplicate the resource sheets.
- Pre-cut cardboard rounds or obtain cardboard circles from a cake decorating shop or a pizza supply source.

Method

Calendars are an important means of counting days, weeks, months, and seasons. Calendars are also a useful way to keep track of time in the church year, often called the liturgical cycle. Review church year information and then make a liturgical calendar in the format of a clock face.

Review the chart with information about each significant time in the church year: day or season, date(s), themes, and colors.

After reviewing the church year information, pick a clock face and use crayons, markers, or colored pencils to fill in the sections with the appropriate colors for important days and seasons. Refer to the chart as a guide in the process.

Cut out the clock face and glue it to the center of a cardboard round. Use the pattern provided for the clock dials, or hands, and trace and cut them from black poster board. Punch holes at the flat, not pointed, ends of the hands and through the center of the clock circle. An awl or compass point works well for this purpose. Push a brass paper fastener through the holes on the layers and then spread the brad from underneath to secure it in place.

Set the clock to the appropriate season. Use the calendar throughout the year, moving the hands as days and seasons change.

Chart for the Church Year

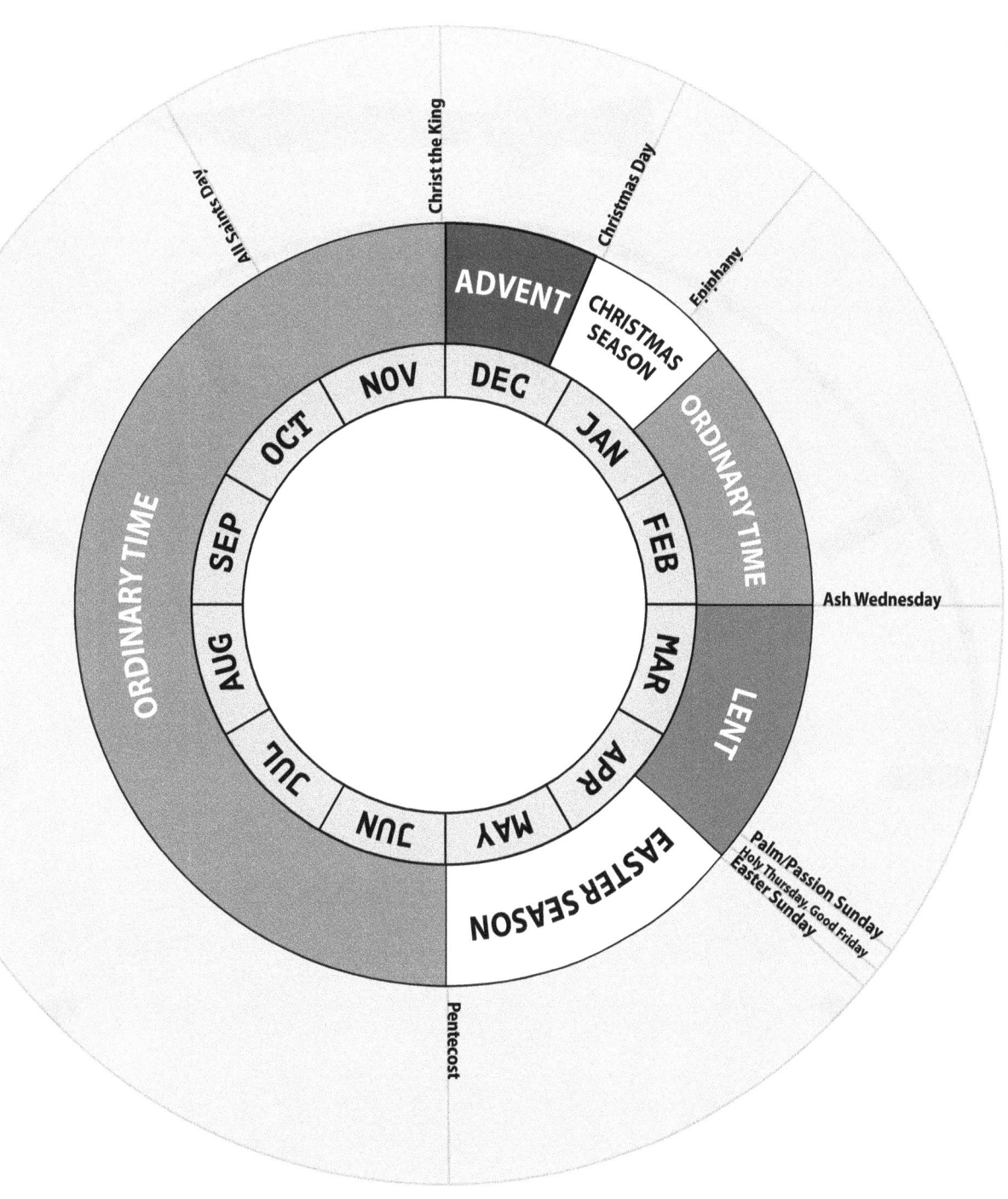

SENSING THE SEASONS: THE CHURCH YEAR

Pattern for Church Year Clock

SENSING THE SEASONS: THE CHURCH YEAR

SENSING THE CHURCH YEAR

Colorful Weavings

Materials

- Baskets or boxes
- Cardboard, 5" x 8" piece for each participant
- Cotton balls or swabs (optional)
- Extracts or essential oils such as almond, cinnamon, clove, lemon, mint, peppermint, and vanilla (optional)
- Knife, utility type
- Markers, permanent
- Materials in church year colors—green, purple, red, white, blue—such as cloth strips, paper pieces, plastic bags, heavy yarns, and wide ribbons
- Resource sheet:
  - Church Year Overview (see Resources section)
- Scissors
- String, heavy

Advance Preparation

- Duplicate the resource sheets.
- Cut the materials into strips one-half inch wide and 10-12 inches long. Place the colored pieces for each season in a separate basket or box.
- Prepare a piece of cardboard for each participant. If available, tablet backs work well for the project.

Method

Weaving is an art form which combines a variety of individual pieces into a beautiful blend of design and texture. Create a weaving to visualize the colors and the symbolism of the seasons of the church year. Use natural materials, such as burlap and cotton, to infuse the project with the smells of the special times.

Select a piece of cardboard to use as the base for the weaving. Prepare the background by cutting one inch slits into the top and bottom. These should be placed approximately one inch apart. Warp the cardboard by running a continuous piece of heavy string from one side to the other, through each slit.

Review the resource sheet highlighting each season of the church year as well as the color and symbolism that is normally associated with it.

Pick a piece of material to represent each season. If desired, print the name of the season on each piece (e.g. write Pentecost on the red strip). An additional, or alternate, idea is to write one thing to remember about each season on each piece of material. A word for Advent might be *coming*, or *prophets*, or *waiting*. Weave the pieces into the base.

Emphasize the sense of smell, as well as sight and touch, by noting the distinct scent of each fabric. Materials like burlap, cotton, linen, polyester, and wool each have a particular odor. Heighten the scent of each segment of the calendar by placing a dab of an extract associated with the smells of the season on the end of the respective pieces (see suggestions on the next page). Use the colorful weaving as a reminder that the story of salvation is woven throughout the cycle of the church year.

	Colors	*Scent Suggestions*
Advent	**Violet** or **purple** represent both the darkness of the world without Christ and the royal purple fit for a king. A bluer purple can be used to distinguish from Lent. The color **blue**, for hope, has been used during this season, too.	**Vanilla** flavor is connected with baking breads, cakes, cookies, and thus anticipation. The smell of **pine oil** can bring to mind Advent wreaths.
Christmas	**White** brings to mind light, joy, and glory during this season.	**Peppermint** is the scent of a candy cane, symbolizing a shepherd's crook.
Epiphany	**White** is also used here, for the light of the star. **Gold** can also represent the star and the gift brought to the Christ child.	**Cloves** can be a reminder of the Magi's gifts of strong spices to the Christ Child. **Frankincense** and **myrrh** represent the gifts, too.
Lent	**Violet** and **purple** remind us of the darkness of our sin, penance, humility, and the royalty of Jesus. On Good Friday the color is sometimes changed to **black** for mourning until Easter Sunday.	**Mint** is associated with the payment of tithes and offerings during Jesus' ministry. **Lavender**, in addition to being purple, is associated with silence, devotion, and calmness.
Easter	**White** focuses us on joy, glory, and triumph of the Resurrection.	**Lemon** symbolizes the movement from sour to sweet, like Jesus' death and resurrection.
Pentecost	**Red** reminds us of the fire of enthusiasm and the force of energy that God's empowerment brings.	**Cinnamon** is a powerful scent with wide reach.
Ordinary Time	**Green** is the color for life and growth.	**Almond** is associated with a process of growth; it is first to blossom but last to bear fruit.

SENSING THE CHURCH YEAR

Bottle Scale Songs

Materials

- Bottles, 8 x 20-ounce containers, clear glass or plastic
- Copy machine or printer
- Dowel rods, 12" lengths
- Food coloring—blue, green, purple, red, yellow
- Markers, permanent
- Measuring cup(s)
- Paper
- Pens
- Plastic tubing, 12" lengths
- Resource sheet: Church Year Songs
- Scissors
- Water

Advance Preparation

- Duplicate the resource sheets.
- Remove the labels from the bottles and wash and dry the containers.
- Decide if the bottles will be prepared in advance or if they will be created as part of the project. Either way, follow these directions to form the musical scale:
  - Gather 8 clear, clean, 20-ounce glass or plastic bottles. Glass produces better sound.
  - With permanent marker, print the name of one church season on each of seven containers and "church year" on the eighth. In addition, print a number on each bottle, beginning with 1 for Advent.
  - Use a measuring cup to fill the eight bottles with the suggested amount of water. Refer to the chart for measurements.
  - To further highlight the symbolism of the seasons, add the appropriate food coloring to the water in each bottle.

Bottle	Season/Feast	Musical Note	Amount of Water	Color
1	Advent	Do	7 ounces	Blue (to distinguish from Lent)
2	Christmas	Re	9 ounces	White (leave clear)
3	Epiphany	Mi	12 ounces	Gold (Yellow)
4	Lent	Fa	14 ounces	Violet/Purple
5	Easter	Sol	16 ounces	White (leave clear)
6	Pentecost	La	17 ounces	Red
7	Ordinary Time	Ti	18 ounces	Green
8	Church Year	Do	19 ounces	White (leave clear)

SENSING THE SEASONS ▪ LEARNING CENTERS FOR THE CHURCH YEAR

Method

Discover the musical qualities of water, and learn about the church year by playing a bottle scale and creating songs to highlight the seasons. Refer to the resource sheet to review the names of the seasons and the liturgical colors associated with them.

Before singing songs or writing words, practice playing a simple tune like "Row, Row, Row Your Boat" on the bottle scale. Playing takes place by blowing into the necks of the bottles or tapping on the sides of the containers.

In order to play the notes, and to keep the tops of the bottles sanitary, pick a new piece of flexible plastic tubing to blow into the necks to create the sound. Because blowing into the bottle causes the air to vibrate, the bottles with the most water in them will make the highest notes. As an alternative, use a dowel rod to tap each bottle to cause the glass to vibrate and produce a sound. In this case, the water dampens the vibrations so the less water in the bottle, the faster the bottle vibrates and the higher the pitch.

The pattern for the first line of "Row, Row, Row Your Boat," whether blowing or tapping, is to blow into or tap bottle number one three times, then bottle number two one time, and finally bottle number three one time. The pattern—that is, the number of blows or taps on a specific bottle number—for the entire song is:

>11123
>32345
>888555333111
>54321

The pattern for "Twinkle, Twinkle Little Star," whether blowing or tapping, is:

>1155665
>4433221
>5544332
>5544332
>1155665
>4433221

Look at the sheet with the sample songs. Try to play the music on the bottle scale and sing the song, too. If more than one person is at the learning center, work together to make the music.

Then take a piece of paper and a pencil and compose church-year related words to sing to the tune "Row, Row, Row Your Boat" or "Twinkle, Twinkle Little Star." If possible, make a second copy of the lyrics—one to leave in the learning center for others to enjoy and one to take home to share with family and friends.

Remember that however the stories of the church year are shared—by playing a bottle scale or singing words to a song—their messages remind us to get ready for the Messiah during Advent, celebrate the birth of the Savior at Christmas, rejoice in God's gift of the Christ Child throughout Epiphany, remember the life and ministry of Jesus in Lent, commemorate the Savior's death and resurrection at Easter, share the Good News of God's love during Pentecost, and grow as disciples throughout Ordinary Time.

Option

Arrange to have the participants share their bottle scale songs at the conclusion of the session.

Sample Church Year Songs

Sing to the tune "Row, Row, Row Your Boat":

**In our church we use a plan
  to teach us God's great story.
Through seasons, symbols, colors, themes
  we live to give God glory.**

Sing to the first two phrases of the tune "Twinkle, Twinkle Little Star."

In the second phrase of the first line of the song, double time the notes on the words "Easter" and "Pentecost" and again for "God's love."

**Advent, Christmas, Epiphany,
Lent, Easter, Pentecost tell God's love for me.**

SENSING THE CHURCH YEAR

Snack Sacks

Materials

- Bags, paper or plastic—2 per participant
- Baskets or containers for treats
- Candy and snacks, individually wrapped, symbolic of church year festivals:
  - Advent—tootsie pops
  - Christmas—candy canes
  - Epiphany—chocolate stars or Starburst
  - Lent—pretzel twists
  - Easter—jelly beans
  - Pentecost—cinnamon red hots
  - Ordinary Time—sunflower seeds
- Pencils or pens
- Resource sheets:
  - Church Year Matching Game
  - Church Year Connections

Advance Preparation

- Duplicate the resource sheets.

Method

The church year helps believers celebrate God's message of love to the world: God's promise of a Savior; Jesus' life, death, and resurrection; and the challenge to share that story with others. Our celebrations are holy days, holidays, or "feasts"—times often associated with favorite tastes. Trace the festivals of faith and connect them with tasty treats as a way to remember the unique message of each season. Then make two snack sacks—one to keep and one to give away—as a way to understand and to share the celebrations of the church year.

Start by playing a matching game to review the festivals of the church year. Take a game sheet and a pencil or pen. Read the names of the festivals on the left side of the paper and the list of descriptions on the right portion of the page. Then draw a line from each festival to the phrase that best describes it. For example, "Epiphany" matches with "Following in faith, offering our gifts to God." Continue until all matches have been made. Before proceeding to the next part of the activity, check answers against the answer key at the bottom of the handout.

Pick up a Church Year Connections chart. Review the names of the festivals in column one. Then, in column two, write a word or a brief description of each of them. For example, the word for "Lent" might be "praying" or "reflecting." Refer to the matching game if ideas are needed.

Use the ideas recorded on the chart to choose a candy or a snack as a way to remember the "reason for each season." Review the treats in the containers: candy canes, chocolate stars or Starbursts, cinnamon red hots, jelly beans, pretzel twists, sunflower seeds, and tootsie pops. Then decide which candy or snack best connects with Advent, Christmas, Epiphany, Lent, Easter, Pentecost, and Ordinary Time. For example, Advent is a time of waiting. Decide which candy best fits with waiting such as waiting for the surprise that is Christmas. Most likely, the response would be the tootsie pop, a hard candy lollipop on the outside filled with chocolate flavored chewy candy on the inside. It takes a lot of licking and sucking—and waiting—to get to the goodness in the middle! Match the name of a candy to the meaning of each season and write the choices on the chart. Then take two paper or plastic bags and prepare snack sacks filled with one of each treat—one bag to enjoy and one to give to someone else.

Conclude by writing a brief explanation of why each candy or snack connects with the meaning of the specific celebration. When the second bag of candy is shared with someone else, explain the reasons to them, too.

In addition to the two snack sacks, take the Matching Game and the Church Year Connections Chart home as reminders of the reasons for the seasons.

Church Year Matching Game

Draw a line to connect the name of each festival of the church year with the phrase that best describes it. Check answers at the bottom of the page.

Festivals	Descriptions
A. Advent	1. Experiencing, practicing, and doing the work of the church in God's world
B. Christmas	2. Rejoicing, accepting God's gift of a Savior
C. Epiphany	3. Celebrating and recognizing the risen Christ
D. Lent	4. Following in faith, offering our gifts to God
E. Easter	5. Welcoming, praising, and sharing the coming of the Holy Spirit
F. Pentecost	6. Waiting, preparing, expecting God's surprise
G. Ordinary Time	7. Praying, appreciating the sacrifice of Love

Answer key: A-6, B-2, C-4, D-7, E-3, F-5, G-1.

SENSING THE SEASONS: THE CHURCH YEAR

Church Year Connections

In the second column, write a word or a brief description of each of the festivals. For example, the word for "Lent" might be "praying" or "reflecting." Use the ideas to choose a candy or a snack as a way to remember the "reason for each season." Which best connects with each season/feast? Write your choices in the third column and a brief explanation of why in the last column.

Festivals	Descriptions	Snacks	Why?
Advent			
Christmas			
Epiphany			
Lent			
Easter			
Pentecost			
Ordinary Time			

SENSING THE SEASONS: THE CHURCH YEAR

SENSING THE CHURCH YEAR

Beaded Pins

Materials

- Beads, glass or plastic—various shapes in church year colors including green, purple, red, and white with option of blue and gold
- Copy machine
- Lectionary or missal (optional)
- Paper for copy machine or printer
- Pencils or pens
- Pins, safety type—medium (size 2) and large (size 3)
- Resource sheets:
  - Church Festivals: Seven for Seven
  - Church Year Overview (see Resources section)

Advance Preparation

- Duplicate the resource sheets.

Method

The two most significant celebrations of the church year are Christmas and Easter. We prepare for Christmas with a four-week period called Advent and get ready for Easter with 40 days known as Lent. Twelve days of Christmas flow into a celebration called Epiphany and fifty days of Easter climax with Pentecost Sunday. In most cases, the rest of the year is called Ordinary Time, which denotes a way of counting the Sundays and weeks between Epiphany and Lent and from Pentecost to Advent.

While this might seem confusing, it is easy to understand that Christians prepare throughout Advent and Lent, celebrate at Christmas and Easter, share during Epiphany and Pentecost, and grow throughout Ordinary Time to begin the cycle again and again, year after year.

One way to remember the important times in the church year is to make beaded pins with festival colors to wear or to put on items. Before making the pins, take time to reflect on the seven main festivals in seven different ways, perhaps one idea each day of the week.

Pick a Church Festivals: 7 for 7 sheet and a pencil or pen. Refer to church calendar materials in the learning center for help with the answers. Fill in all of the colors and take the sheet home to complete during the specific times in the church year. The seven topics to think about are:

- Festival/Season
- Date or time period (e.g. Epiphany: Jan. 6)
- Bible stories (e.g. Christmas: Angels appear to shepherds)
- Special days (e.g. Lent: Palm Sunday)

- Color(s)
- Symbols (e.g. Pentecost: wind)
- Why is it important? (e.g. Advent: God promised a Savior)

Complete portions of the sheet and set it aside to take home to use throughout the year.

Create a beaded pin. For a simple project, select a medium-size safety pin and open it. Pick seven beads—one representing each color of the significant times in the church year. In addition, the seven beads can serve as a reminder of seven ways to think about the church calendar. Arrange the beads in a pattern, for example violet/blue for Advent, white for Christmas, white or gold for Epiphany, purple for Lent, white for Easter, red for Pentecost, and green for Ordinary Time. Place the beads on the open pin in order of the pattern. Close the pin. To display or wear the decoration, carefully attach it to a backpack or book bag, item of clothing, hat, or shoes.

For a more challenging activity, combine one large and seven medium safety pins for the project. Begin by making seven single beaded pins. In this case, each pin represents one important time in the church year. On the first pin, for Advent, thread seven blue or purple beads or combine the two colors in the design. Continue by beading a separate pin for Christmas, Epiphany, Lent, Easter, Pentecost, and Ordinary Time. Next, open a large pin and loop the bottom of the seven completed pins onto it. The large pin will loop through the holes on the bottom of the medium safety pins. Carefully close the large pin. The seven beaded pins now dangle from the larger pin. Wear the pin or display it on special items.

If there are enough supplies, make additional pins to give as gifts and to trade with others.

Church Festivals: 7 for 7 (1/2)

	Date/Time Period	Bible stories	Special days	Colors	Symbols	Why is it important?
Advent						
Christmas						
Epiphany						

SENSING THE SEASONS: THE CHURCH YEAR

Church Festivals: 7 for 7 (2/2)

	Date/Time Period	Bible stories	Special days	Colors	Symbols	Why is it important?
Lent						
Easter						
Pentecost						
Ordinary Time						

SENSING THE SEASONS: THE CHURCH YEAR

Sensing Advent

Isaiah 11:1-3a

> *A shoot shall come out from the stump of Jesse, and a branch shall grow out of his roots. The spirit of the Lord shall rest on him, the spirit of wisdom and understanding, the spirit of counsel and might, the spirit of knowledge and the fear of the Lord. His delight shall be in the fear of the Lord.*

Advent is the season of preparation for the coming of Christ, beginning in late November or early December—four Sundays prior to Christmas Day, December 25th. During Advent, the church prepares for the birth of Jesus as a babe in a manger in history and for the rebirth of Christ's presence in the hearts of faithful people. As well, Advent is a time to remember that we also wait for Christ's promised return to the world, called the Second Coming. Scripture readings focus on prophecy, especially Isaiah's foretelling of the Messiah's coming and John the Baptist's announcement of the need for repentance and preparation for the One who is to come.

God started preparing the world for Jesus' birth thousands of years ago. When God saw that people were not able to find their way through the darkness of sin and selfishness, God provided prophets, or messengers, to let people know that God had a plan. The prophets foretold of Jesus' coming many centuries before his birth. That way, people understood that there was hope. God had not given up on human beings, but would provide a way of salvation. Even though we live in the time after Jesus came to earth, human beings still get lost in the darkness of sin and selfishness. Advent symbolizes that we wait for the re-birth of hope, just like the prophets did. We remember that God has a plan for us, too. As we prepare our minds and hearts for Jesus' re-birth, we review our need for God's salvation and open our lives to God's Messiah, the Chosen One who will show us the way through the darkness. Advent is a time to get ready on the inside so that God's love will shine through our lives and make a difference on the outside.

The color for Advent is usually violet or purple, representing both the darkness of the world without Christ and the royal purple fit for a king. The color blue, for hope, has been employed during this season, too. If an Advent wreath is used, purple or blue candles are lit, one each week signifying that the light of Christ is coming closer. Traditionally, the third candle is pink to signify joy. On Christmas Day, and/or Christmas Eve, a white Christ candle can be lit to announce the birth of Jesus, the Light of the World.

SENSING ADVENT

Decorated Candles

Materials

- Brushes for glue
- Candles, small votive
- Containers for glue mixture
- Glasses, heavy juice size
- Glitter, opalescent or white
- Glue, white
- Napkins or tissue paper with holiday designs
- Newspaper or plates
- Scissors

Method

Candles glow throughout Advent as a symbol for Jesus, the light of the world. Create small decorative candles to enhance holiday decor or to give as holiday gifts.

Cut seasonal pictures from gift wrap or paper napkins. Be sure that the designs are in proportion to the glass.

Pour a small amount of glue into the container and thin with a little water. Brush glue onto the outside of the glass votive candle and attach each paper design. Carefully position the paper shapes while the glue is wet. Then gently brush the glue mixture over the entire outer surface of the paper and glass to be sure the designs are fastened. Smooth away any bubbles or wrinkles.

Place fingers of the left hand, if right-handed, inside the glass and spread them to hold the glass firmly. With the other hand, sprinkle glitter over glued surface. Rotate the glass to cover the sides completely. Place newspaper or a plate under the glass to catch excess glitter. Tap the glass to remove loose glitter particles.

Place the glass on a non-stick surface, such as a plate, to dry. Add the votive candle.

To use the decoration, be aware that there could be glitter near the bottom of the candle holder, so use a coaster or other protection to keep from marring furniture. Also when the votive burns down, add another candle to prevent the glass from getting too hot and potentially breaking.

Throughout the entire project, use caution with glass and be mindful of candle safety!

SENSING ADVENT

Lavender Sachets

Materials

- Cotton balls or polyfil
- Envelopes, small
- Hole punch
- Ink pads, purple
- Lavender, dried flowers and/or oil
- Markers, fine tips
- Measuring spoon, teaspoon
- Ribbon
- Rubber stamps
- Scissors

Method

Advent is a time of waiting for the coming of the Messiah. This period of preparation begins with quiet contemplation and progresses to the excitement of Christmas Day. Arrange for calm, reflective moments in order to sense all aspects of the season.

For centuries, the scent made from oils and flowers of the aromatic lavender plant has been used to calm and to soothe. Lavender is a favorite fragrance found in bath soaps, perfumes, and sachets.

Make fragrant lavender sachets with purple stamped designs as reminders to include peaceful times during the Advent season. Decorate several small envelopes, invitation size or smaller, with rubber stamps and purple ink. Choose stamps with symbols appropriate for the season such as angels, borders, candles, stars, and vines. Punch a hole in one corner of each envelope.

Gather several cotton balls or polyfil for each sachet, dot with a few drops of lavender oil, and place in a prepared envelope. If dried flowers are used, place one tablespoon of the mixture in each envelope. Seal the flap and tie a ribbon loop through the hole.

To use the sachet, place it under a pillow or in a drawer or hang it in the closet. Enjoy a "whiff" of Advent while going about the daily routine.

SENSING ADVENT

Music Mobiles

Materials

- Crayons or markers
- Equipment to play music
- Hangers
- Hole punch
- Music for selected songs
- Paper, construction or poster board
- Resource materials on hymn stories
- Ribbon or yarn
- Scissors

Method

Music is a traditional part of waiting and celebrating Advent. Learn more about the songs of the season and make mobiles to symbolize their stories. Decide which Advent carols to use and find information about them. "O Come, O Come Emmanuel" is a good one for the project.

Cut four shapes from construction paper or poster board. The shapes may help represent the message or symbolism of the music. Write the following information on three of the pieces: composer and biographical information; history of the carol; title and words. On the fourth shape, draw an illustration of the message of the song.

Punch a hole at the top of each shape and string a length of ribbon or yarn through it. Tie the four pieces to various sections of the hanger. Enjoy both the music and the message during the Advent season.

SENSING ADVENT
Cookie Gifts

Materials

- Art materials for decorating the containers
- Containers for cookies such as plastic tubs
- Cookie cutters—animal shapes
- Equipment and utensils including cookie sheets, rolling pins, and knives
- Frosting and gel tubes
- Gift tags
- Ingredients for cookie recipe
- Oven
- Paper, waxed
- Pens or markers
- Plates
- Sprinkles and sugars for decorating cookies

Advance Preparation

Prepare cookies beforehand if time is limited.

Recipe for Brown Sugar Crisps

Ingredients:

- 1 teaspoon baking powder
- ¼ teaspoon baking soda
- 1½ cups light brown sugar, firmly packed
- 1¼ cups (2½ sticks) butter or margarine
- 2 eggs
- 4 cups sifted all-purpose flour
- 1 teaspoon maple extract
- 1 teaspoon salt

Instructions:

- Sift flour, baking powder, baking soda, and salt together. Cream butter or margarine and sugar; add maple extract and eggs.
- Beat well. Add flour mixture, beating until blended.
- Place cookie dough in a bowl or form it into a log, or two, and chill in refrigerator at least one hour.

Method

Baking is a big part of holiday preparations. The expectation of Advent can be represented by the simple act of waiting for bread dough to rise or cookie dough to chill. People eagerly anticipate tasting the finished product.

Using the dough that was prepared in advance, cut, roll, bake, and decorate cookies to give as gifts—and to sample as well.

Cut two sheets of waxed paper. Prepare one as the work surface by sprinkling flour on it. Set a portion of dough on the sheet and flatten it slightly with the hand. Position the second piece of waxed paper on top of the dough. Use a rolling pin to roll the dough to a ¼ inch thickness. If the dough was formed in a log, cut it into ¼ inch slices and flatten it with the hand or a rolling pin.

Remove top sheet of waxed paper. Dip cookie cutters in flour and cut shapes from the dough. If desired, decorate the cookies with colored sugar or sprinkles. Transfer to a greased cookie sheet. Bake in 350° oven for 8-10 minutes or until cookies are golden in color.

While the cookies are baking, use this "waiting time" to decorate the containers and the gift tags. Choose from the art materials provided to draw symbols and to write words on the cartons and the cards.

Once the cookies have baked, transfer them to a wire rack to cool completely. Continue decorating, if desired, putting each on a plate and adding frosting, gel, and additional trims.

Enjoy the taste of the warm cookies. Fill the decorated containers with treats to share with family and friends.

SENSING ADVENT

Mini Wreaths

Materials

- Candle lighter or matches (optional)
- Candles, small to medium birthday type—blue, pink, purple, white
- Coasters or small paper doilies
- Glue
- Pans, foil—tart size
- Play dough, homemade or purchased—green
- Ribbon, narrow—blue, pink, purple, white
- Rings from canning jars
- Toothpicks

Advance Preparation

- Gather all materials.

Method

In many churches, homes, and schools, an Advent wreath is a focal point during this special season. The varied textures of the arrangement can add to its beauty: bristly evergreens, waxy candles, silky ribbons, and smooth candlesticks.

Enjoy a tactile experience by modeling green play dough to make a tiny Advent wreath out of a canning jar ring. Take a small portion—golf ball size—of green play dough. Knead, roll, and pinch the dough to enjoy its texture. Press the play dough onto a canning jar ring, covering the metal surface. To simulate the texture of evergreen needles, use a toothpick to press lines into the dough.

Push four small candles, birthday cake size, into the wreath before the dough hardens. Choose colors according to the tradition followed in the church or the family, if possible (normally three purple or blue candles plus one pink candle). Position the wreath on top of a beverage coaster or a paper doily. Place everything on a "bottom up" foil tart pan, which will serve as a base.

Roll a small ball of dough to hold the Christ candle. Push a white medium-sized birthday candle into the ball and press it firmly into the center of the base.

Allow the dough to harden, then add small bows made of narrow ribbon to the wreath. If the desired Advent colors are not available, tie ribbon of an appropriate color around each candle near the base.

When the candles are lighted, use extreme caution with candle lighters or matches and flames!

Sensing Christmas

Isaiah 9:6-7

> *For a child has been born for us, a son given to us; authority rests upon his shoulders; and he is named Wonderful Counselor, Mighty God, Everlasting Father, Prince of Peace. His authority shall grow continually, and there shall be endless peace for the throne of David and his kingdom. He will establish and uphold it with justice and with righteousness from this time onward and forevermore. The zeal of the Lord of hosts will do this.*

Christmas is the season beginning on December 25th. Traditionally 12 days, it extends somewhat longer in some traditions. As carols are sung, the Christmas story read, and the birth of Christ celebrated, Christians rejoice that God sent us the promised Messiah in the form of a tiny baby named Jesus. Jesus is the fulfillment of a promise that God made hundreds of years earlier. God, who formed the universe and who was saddened to see creation fall, designed a plan for redemption through the birth, life, death, and resurrection of Jesus. We learn in Advent that the prophets told people to get ready because a Messiah was coming, the Chosen One of Israel who would lead God's people to find hope and peace. In the Christmas season, we have the opportunity to share again and again the joy of knowing that God faithfully kept the promise to send a Savior, and we know him to be Jesus! Jesus—God-in-flesh—came to earth to bring hope, to show us the way, and to be the Way. The challenge of Christmas is to appreciate the humanity of Jesus who was born as a baby in Bethlehem and to worship the divine Jesus who conquered death and sin for us.

Scripture passages related to the story of Jesus' birth and the events that preceded and followed it include Matthew 1 and 2, Luke 1 and 2, and John 1:1-14. Numerous Old Testament references anticipate the coming of the Messiah and many New Testament verses confirm Christ as the Savior of the world. Each reading or telling of the Christmas story invites us to recognize anew that we are the ones who need the Savior, we are the ones whom "God so loved." At Christmas we must open our hearts to the re-birth of the joy of knowing that Christ came to be our Savior.

The color for Christmas is usually white, the color reserved for the holiest festivals of the church year.

Stained Glass Ornaments

Materials

- Cord
- Glue sticks
- Paper, construction—black
- Paper, tissue in bright colors
- Paper, waxed
- Scissors
- Tape

Method

Beautiful sights during the holidays include jewel-toned stained glass windows depicting scenes from the Christmas story. Besides being the focal point of exquisite displays, these brilliant images often appear on greeting cards, gift wrap, and holiday decorations. As a keepsake of the season, make simple stained glass ornaments from construction paper and colored tissue paper to use at church, home, or school, or to give as gifts.

Cut a full sheet of black construction paper into four equal pieces. Fold each quarter sheet in half to use as the base of a stained glass ornament. Use scissors to cut openings along the fold line, similar to making a snowflake. Then carefully poke a scissor point into the paper on each side of the fold line to cut additional openings. The more cutouts there are, the more colorful the ornament will be when the colors fill the spaces.

Cut tissue paper pieces slightly larger than each opening on the ornament. Position a piece of tissue over each hole. Then use a glue stick to attach the tissue to the construction paper shape. Once the tissue is in place, cut a piece of waxed paper to fit the ornament. Tape the waxed paper behind the glued tissue to help hold the shapes in place. Attach a cord loop as a hanger.

To use the ornament, display it in a window so the jewel-like colors will appear.

Pomander Balls

Materials

- Allspice
- Awls or skewers
- Bags, plastic
- Cheesecloth (optional)
- Cinnamon
- Cloves, whole
- Cord
- Flowers, small silk (optional)
- Glue
- Measuring spoons
- Oranges, firm
- Orris root (a preservative found in spice aisle of grocery store or at drug or herb store)
- Pins, straight
- Ribbon
- Scissors

Method

The aromatic combination of citrus and spice is a traditional scent of Christmas in baked goods, potpourri, seasonings, and teas. Pomander balls, constructed from cloves, other spices, and oranges, make a fragrant and welcome gift. For hundreds of years people have used them to freshen the air, to fight illness, and even to discourage moths.

For each creation, use a firm orange, mandarin, or tangerine, two to three ounces of whole cloves, one tablespoon of ground cinnamon, and two teaspoons of ground orris root which serves as a preservative. If orris root is omitted, add more cinnamon or a half teaspoon of allspice.

Use an awl or skewer to punch holes in the orange skin. A random pattern works best; too many holes in a straight line might cause a split in the skin. Insert whole cloves into the pre-punched pattern, covering most of the surface of the orange.

Mix the ground spices in a plastic bag, then place the fruit into the bag and seal or twist the top to close it. Gently shake the clove-studded orange to coat it with the other spices.

Give the piece its finishing touches. Tie a ribbon around the orange, overlap the ends at the top, and pin; tie a second ribbon crossing over the first ribbon at the top, overlap the two ends at the bottom, and pin. Push additional straight pins in at the bottom and the top to secure the criss-crossed ribbons. Attach a cord for hanging. Glue on a bow or dried flowers for a more decorative finish.

In order to keep the citrus from getting moldy and to use it for a week or more, display the ball during the day but place it in the refrigerator at night. For best results, and indefinite use, tie the fruit into a square of cheesecloth allowing air to circulate around it. Hang the bag in a cool, dry place so the orange will shrink and become hard. This process will sustain the fruit, and the scent, for much longer.

Mini Jingle Bell Wreaths

Materials

- Bells, jingle-type
- Needles
- Pony tail holders, ruffled—shades of green
- Ribbon, plaid or red
- Scissors
- Thread, heavy—green

Method

One of the favorite sounds of Christmas is the happy music of jingle bells. During the season, they might ring on holiday jewelry, household decorations, or even sleigh rides! Make a jingle bell wreath to wear or to attach to a door knob to add music to the symphony of Christmas.

Select a green ruffled pony tail holder to use as the base of a wreath. Using double or heavy thread, sew jingle bells all over the cloth. Arrange the bells in clusters or scatter them around the material. Add small or large bows by sewing them to the fabric, too.

Stretch the jingle bell-covered elastic to fit around a door knob, to encircle the wrist, or to dress up a ponytail. The jingle bell wreath will become part of the sounds of the season.

Gingerbread with Toppings

Materials

- Bowl for each topping (two total)
- Equipment and utensils, including forks and knives
- Ingredients in recipes
- Oven
- Napkins
- Plates
- Recipe, or cake mix, for gingerbread

Advance Preparation

- Make gingerbread from a mix or a recipe prior to the session. Once baked and cooled, place two cookies or a square of cake on separate plates and set them on the table for the activity. If time permits, make the gingerbread during the session.
- Prepare each topping—cream cheese and lemon sauce—before the session. Place a bowl of each, along with knifes or spoons, on the activity table. If time permits, make both toppings during the session.

Recipe for Cream Cheese Topping

Ingredients:

- 3 ounce package cream cheese
- Few drops of lemon juice
- 1 teaspoon lemon rind, grated
- 3 Tablespoons milk
- 1 Tablespoon sugar

Instructions:

- Combine ingredients and put in bowl.
- Store in refrigerator until ready to serve.

Recipe for Lemon Sauce

Ingredients:

- 2 Tablespoons butter
- 1 Tablespoon cornstarch
- 3 Tablespoons lemon juice, fresh
- 1 teaspoon lemon rind
- ¼ teaspoon salt
- ½ cup sugar
- ½ teaspoon vanilla
- ¾ cup boiling water
- ¼ cup cold water

Instructions:

- Combine sugar, cornstarch, and salt.
- Mix in cold water.
- Gradually stir in boiling water and cook for three minutes or until smooth, clear, and slightly thickened.
- Add remaining ingredients. Makes about 1½ cups. Serve cold or warm.

Method

A familiar taste of Christmas is gingerbread. This favorite dessert may appear as cake, cookies, or even a decorative house. For a new taste treat, try gingerbread with a tasty cream cheese topping or a tangy lemon sauce.

Select a plate of gingerbread—cake or cookies—to enjoy. Sample either or both of the toppings. Use a knife or a spoon to cover the gingerbread with the cream cheese spread and/or the lemon sauce. Savor a taste of Christmas while relishing the dessert.

SENSING CHRISTMAS

Evergreen Prints

Materials

- Books, heavy, or irons (optional)
- Brushes
- Clean up supplies
- Evergreen branches, small
- Newspaper
- Paint, acrylic
- Paper, butcher paper—brown, if possible
- Paper, card stock
- Paper, scrap
- Pencils
- Scissors

Advance Preparation

- Gather small evergreen branches from bushes or a Christmas tree. Blue spruce, cedar, juniper, or yew work well for this project. If necessary, flatten branches between several sheets of newspaper which are weighted down with heavy books or irons. Evergreens that are less bulky and a little flatter will produce a clearer print.

Method

The Christmas season would not seem complete without the distinctive fragrance and the varied texture of evergreens. Some branches feel prickly while others seem silky, yet all can be used to create distinctive painted prints.

Decide on an item to make such as a bookmark, greeting card, picture, or wrapping paper. For a bookmark, cut card stock to the desired size; a card, fold a sheet of card stock in half; a picture, use the entire piece. For wrapping paper, cut butcher paper to the size needed to wrap a gift.

Choose an evergreen bough that will fit on the prepared paper. Experiment with the process on scrap paper to find the right color and the correct amount of paint to use. Brush paint on one side of the evergreen branch; firmly press onto the paper. After printing, lift the branch carefully to prevent lines from smudging. When confident with the technique, use it to create the desired items.

Embellish the evergreen prints. Make fingerprint dots for berries or paint tiny pine cones for added interest. Allow the paint to dry. Enjoy the textured evergreen prints and make extras to give as gifts.

Option

In addition to paper projects, cloth items such as aprons, place mats, sweatshirts, and t-shirts would work well with this project. If desired, contact the participants in advance and invite them to bring an item to paint. For cloth articles, use fabric paint and follow directions on the containers.

Sensing Epiphany

Matthew 2:11

> *On entering the house, they saw the child with Mary his mother; and they knelt down and paid him homage. Then, opening their treasure chests, they offered him gifts of gold, frankincense, and myrrh.*

Epiphany falls on January 6th, following immediately after the twelve days of Christmas (although it is often observed on the closest Sunday). In some churches, Epiphany is celebrated as a season that continues until the beginning of Lent, although others observe a season of winter Ordinary Time.

Epiphany literally means appearance or revelation. Other words to describe this time in the church year include manifestation or showing forth. At this time, Christians celebrate the arrival of the Magi from the East to the Christ Child in Bethlehem, signifying that God has been revealed to all the nations in Jesus. These travelers saw the star that foretold this birth and they followed its light until they found the special child God had sent. The fact that they came from far away and from different cultures was God's way of revealing that the Savior was for everyone who believes and follows, not just a chosen few.

The Magi are often called the Three Wise Men or Kings, but the Bible does not record their number (we only know there were three *gifts*) or royalty status. In fact, the Greek word that Matthew uses for them does not even reveal their gender. Magi were Zoroastrian priests known for astrology and dream interpretation, and many at the time were women.

Epiphany also celebrates that Jesus didn't stay a small child, but grew to be a man who had a mission to fulfill for God. At Jesus' baptism, God revealed that Jesus was the Son of God. Epiphany reminds us that Jesus was born to save the world. The season of Epiphany is a time of celebrating new revelations of God's presence among us.

For the Festival of Epiphany the appropriate color is white, although gold is sometimes used as the color of the star and the gift brought to the Christ Child.

SENSING EPIPHANY

Sand Painted Cards

Materials

- Bags, small paper or plastic or containers—one for each color of sand
- Cardboard
- Glue
- Newspaper
- Paint, tempera
- Paper, card stock
- Paper, scrap
- Pencils
- Sand
- Scissors
- Tape

Advance Preparation

- Obtain clean sand from a craft or home store.
- If desired, it can be colored by mixing a small amount of tempera paint into it and kneading it thoroughly. Spread the sand on newspaper to dry. Stir it from time to time to separate the particles. Place each color into its own small paper or plastic bag or individual container.
- Colored sand for the project may also be purchased.

Method

Create a picture for the front of an Epiphany card by combining different colors of sand to form a design. Sand is an appropriate material to use for this project since the Magi might have traveled through sandy deserts to reach the Christ Child.

Decide on a symbol to use on the cover of the card such as a crown, a gift container, or a star. Sketch the picture for the card on a piece of scrap paper. Plan the colors of the project according to the materials that have been gathered.

Select a sheet of card stock paper and fold it in half to serve as the card. Then cut a piece of cardboard to a size that will fit inside of the cover of the card.

Transfer the sketch on the paper to the cardboard. Choose an area to be covered with a single color of sand. Spread white glue over the section. Sprinkle the desired color of sand over the glue. Allow the glue to dry. Hold the cardboard over the bag or container from which the sand was taken. Tap the picture lightly so the loose sand falls into the bag. Glue another small area and follow the same procedure. Continue until the painting is completed.

Glue or tape the back of the sand painting to the front of the card. Use a pen to write an Epiphany message inside—something that connects with the design on the card. Give or send the greeting to someone who will enjoy receiving it.

Incense Holders

Materials

- Bags, small plastic
- Cord, gold
- Incense
- Glue, tacky or hot glue gun and glue sticks
- Pans, foil mini-tart size
- Pens
- Stars, foil or garland
- Tags for gifts

Advance Preparation

- Purchase incense made from balsam to best represent the fragrance of frankincense. It can be found at stores that carry candles or potpourri, in gift shops, and at some super markets.

Method

Frankincense is a fragrant gum-resin used as a perfume, as a medicine, and in religious rites. It was reported to be one of the treasured gifts the Magi brought to Jesus. Create an incense holder to add to a family holiday tradition or to give as an Epiphany, or Twelfth Night, gift.

Select a small foil tart pan. Prepare the incense holder by putting a line of glue all around the top edge of the pan. Press garland with stars or individual foil stars into the glue. Add additional stars to the sides of the pan. Place incense in the center of the star-studded tart pan. When ready to use, light according to package directions.

Make individual gift packs by assembling a decorated tart pan and several pieces of incense in a small plastic bag. Tie gold cord around the end of the bag and write a wish that those who use the gift will enjoy the scents of Epiphany as the fragrance fills the air. Provide lighting instructions with the gift as well.

SENSING EPIPHANY

Sound Effects

Materials

- Bible
- Digital sound recorder or phone with video
- Objects for sound effects such as can with lid, cork, crinkly fabric, glass bottle, metal box, pie plate, plastic glasses, stones

Method

Think about the sounds associated with the story of Epiphany. Take time to review the Bible passage, Matthew 2:1-12, to recall the possibilities. Auditory remembrances could include the clopping feet of camels, the chattering noises of busy marketplaces, and the babbling of a young child. They might also involve the rustling of regal Magi robes, the opening of gift boxes, and the bells on the tack of the camels.

Make sound effects from ordinary, household items to add to a scripture script. Try some of these suggestions and make up others as well:

- Birds singing: Rub a wet cork over the side of a glass bottle.
- Gifts: Open and close a metal container with a lid.
- Hooves: Use two sturdy plastic glasses. Knock one end, then the other of one glass down on a table top. "Clop" the second glass after the other. Increase the speed.
- Marching feet: Put several stones inside a tin can, place the lid on the container, and shake the stones up and down.
- Movement of Magi: Rustle crinkly fabric.
- Rain: Scatter uncooked pasta or rice, or small pebbles, in the bottom of a pie pan and move them around.

Select several sound effects to add to a unique version of the story of the visit to the Christ Child and record it as a special remembrance of Epiphany. Read the story out loud, add the noises, and make a keepsake of it with a digital recorder or a video on a phone.

Crisp Rice Star Treats

Materials

- Candies or sprinkles
- Cookie cutters, star shapes
- Cooking spray
- Equipment and utensils including cookie sheets and knives
- Frosting, canned, or decorating gel
- Ingredients for crisp rice cookies
- Plates
- Napkins
- Recipe for crisp rice cookies (Provided)

Advance Preparation

- If time is a factor, make a pan of crisp rice cookies in advance.

Recipe for Crisp Rice Treats

Ingredients:

- 3 Tablespoons butter or margarine
- 4 cups miniature marshmallows
- 6 cups crisp rice cereal

Instructions:

- Grease a cookie sheet or coat it with cooking spray.
- In a large saucepan melt butter over low heat. Add marshmallows and stir until completely melted. Remove from heat. Add crisp rice cereal. Stir until well coated.
- Press mixture into cookie sheet. Cool.

Method

Matthew 2:1-2, 7, 9-10 records the story of the star that led the Magi from the East to the town of Bethlehem to find the Christ Child:

In the time of King Herod, after Jesus was born in Bethlehem of Judea, wise men from the East came to Jerusalem, asking, 'Where is the child who has been born king of the Jews? For we observed his star at its rising, and have come to pay him homage.' Then Herod secretly called for the wise men and learned from them the exact time when the star had appeared. When they had heard the king, they set out; and there, ahead of them, went the star that they had seen at its rising, until it stopped over the place where the child was. When they saw that the star had stopped, they were overwhelmed with joy.

Since the star is such a prominent part of the story of Epiphany, enjoy a treat in the shape of this important symbol.

Use a star-shaped cookie cutter, coated with cooking spray, to cut a symbol—or two—from a batch of crisp rice cereal treats. Set the cookies on a plate. Use the frosting, gels, and candies provided to decorate the treat. Enjoy.

SENSING EPIPHANY

Shell Covered Chests

Materials

- Boxes, cigar or other sturdy type with lids
- Brushes, paint
- Cord or trim
- Glue, tacky, or glue guns with glue sticks
- Paint, acrylic, gesso, or spray
- Pans or trays
- Pencils
- Scissors
- Shells, assorted
- Toothpicks
- Tweezers

Advance Preparation

- Cover the boxes with a coat of acrylic, gesso, or spray paint so they will be dry before the activity.
- Place shells in pans or trays.

Method

Matthew 2:11 states that the travelers from the East, called the Magi, brought the Christ Child gifts of gold, frankincense, and myrrh. Create a chest, adorned with shells, suitable for royalty to share.

Select a pre-painted box with a lid to use for the project. Pick a variety of shells and create a simple, yet striking, arrangement on the cover. The design can be a specific motif or a random pattern made from flat, dish-like clam type shells or cone-shaped, spiral snail shells. Affix each shell, one by one, to the box top with tacky glue. Toothpicks and tweezers often help in handling tiny shells. For large shells, use a glue gun with caution, to attach the pieces.

For a finished look, glue heavy cord or other trims around the outside edge of the lid.

Use care when moving the box until the glue is completely dry.

Sensing Lent

John 3:16

> *For God so loved the world that he gave his only Son, so that everyone who believes in him may not perish but may have eternal life.*

Like Advent, Lent is a season of preparation. Historically in the church, it was the time set aside for new converts to prepare for baptism or for other Christians to do penance and be restored. The 40 days prior to Easter were dedicated to fasting, prayer, and self-examination. However, Sundays were to be treated as "little Easters" when the fast and penance could be set aside to celebrate Jesus' victory. Hence, there are really 46 days in this period.

Ash Wednesday marks the beginning of the time of preparation. In some churches, last year's palms are burned and mixed with oil and the mixture is placed on the foreheads of the faithful as a sign of humility. The Sunday before Easter is often called Palm Sunday to commemorate Jesus' triumphant entry into Jerusalem and the beginning of Holy Week with the events that led up to the crucifixion. Some churches call the Sunday one week before Easter Passion Sunday to remember specifically the extreme suffering that Jesus experienced on the cross. The waiting of Lent is finally over with the arrival of Holy Thursday (Maundy Thursday), which calls for a celebration of the institution of the Last Supper, the Passover Seder meal Jesus shared with his disciples. Good Friday is a paradoxical celebration of Jesus' death: while the suffering of crucifixion can hardly be called good, the gift of salvation through Christ's sacrifice is Good News for the Christian. Finally, we celebrate Easter Sunday and the joy of Resurrection.

The focus of the Scripture readings during Lent present the 40 days Jesus spent in the desert after his baptism preparing for ministry and being tested by Satan. During this time as well, the church proclaims the Transfiguration story, accounts of Jesus' encounters with religious leaders, and passages that relate Jesus' awareness of his mission and its consequences. The Christian's challenge to spend 40 days in reflection and spiritual discipline parallels the message of the season.

The color for Lent is again purple, a color reminding us of the darkness of our sin and the royalty of Jesus. On Good Friday the color black is sometimes used to symbolize mourning. Sometimes an early sunrise service on Easter marks the transition from darkness to light, replacing black with white.

SENSING LENT

Cross Symbols

Materials

- Clothesline, elastic cords with hook ends, or rope (optional)
- Clothes pins, glue, or straight pins (optional)
- Copy machine or printer
- Hole punch
- Markers, fine point or pens
- Paper, cardstock—white
- Paper for printer
- Resource sheets:
  - Types of Crosses
  - Cross Patterns
- Ribbon, narrow purple—various shades
- Scissors

Advance Preparation

- Cut clothesline or rope into 12-18 pieces, one per participant.
- Cut ribbon into 12 inch pieces.
- Duplicate the resource sheets.

Method

Lent is a season of reflection before the celebration of Easter. Throughout this period the focus should be on the cross. In order to keep this important emblem "in sight," create a personal display featuring different styles of crosses.

Review the resource sheet on types of crosses and read the explanations about them. Keep in mind that the crosses on the sheet offer a sample of the styles that have developed through the years. Using the cross patterns provided, use a pair of scissors to cut out the shapes. Instead of cutting the intricate parts of some of the styles, cut each design into the shape of a circle or an oval. With fine-tipped marker or a pen, print the name of each cross on the shape.

Punch a small hole at the top of each cross. For each completed symbol, select a piece of narrow purple ribbon, thread it through the hole, and tie it at the top of the cardstock. Leave the two pieces of ribbon to hang so they can be tied to a display.

If clothesline, rope, or an elastic cord is available, select one piece and tie the cross symbols to it. To keep the decorations from moving, place a dot of glue, a straight pin, or a clothespin at the top of each ribbon. If cord is not available, take the decorations home and display them in windows, attach them to a wreath, or hang them from light fixtures—anywhere that will keep the cross "in sight" during the season of Lent.

Types of Crosses

Celtic Cross

A Greek or Latin cross, with a circle enclosing the intersection of the upright and crossbar

Maltese Cross

An eight-pointed cross having the form of four "V"-shaped elements, each joining the others at its vertex, leaving the other two tips spread outward symmetrically.

Greek Cross

Cross with arms of equal length

St. Andrew's Cross

An X-shaped cross.

Jerusalem Cross

A large cross with a smaller cross in each of its angles. Also called a Crusader's Cross.

Stepped Cross

Cross resting on a base with three steps. Also called Calvary Cross or Graded Cross.

Latin Cross

Cross with a longer descending arm. Also called a Roman cross.

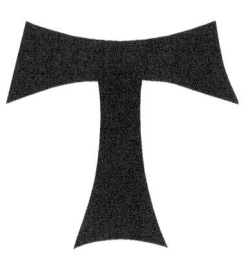

Tau Cross

A T-shaped cross. Also called a St. Anthony Cross or St. Francis Cross.

SENSING THE SEASONS: LENT

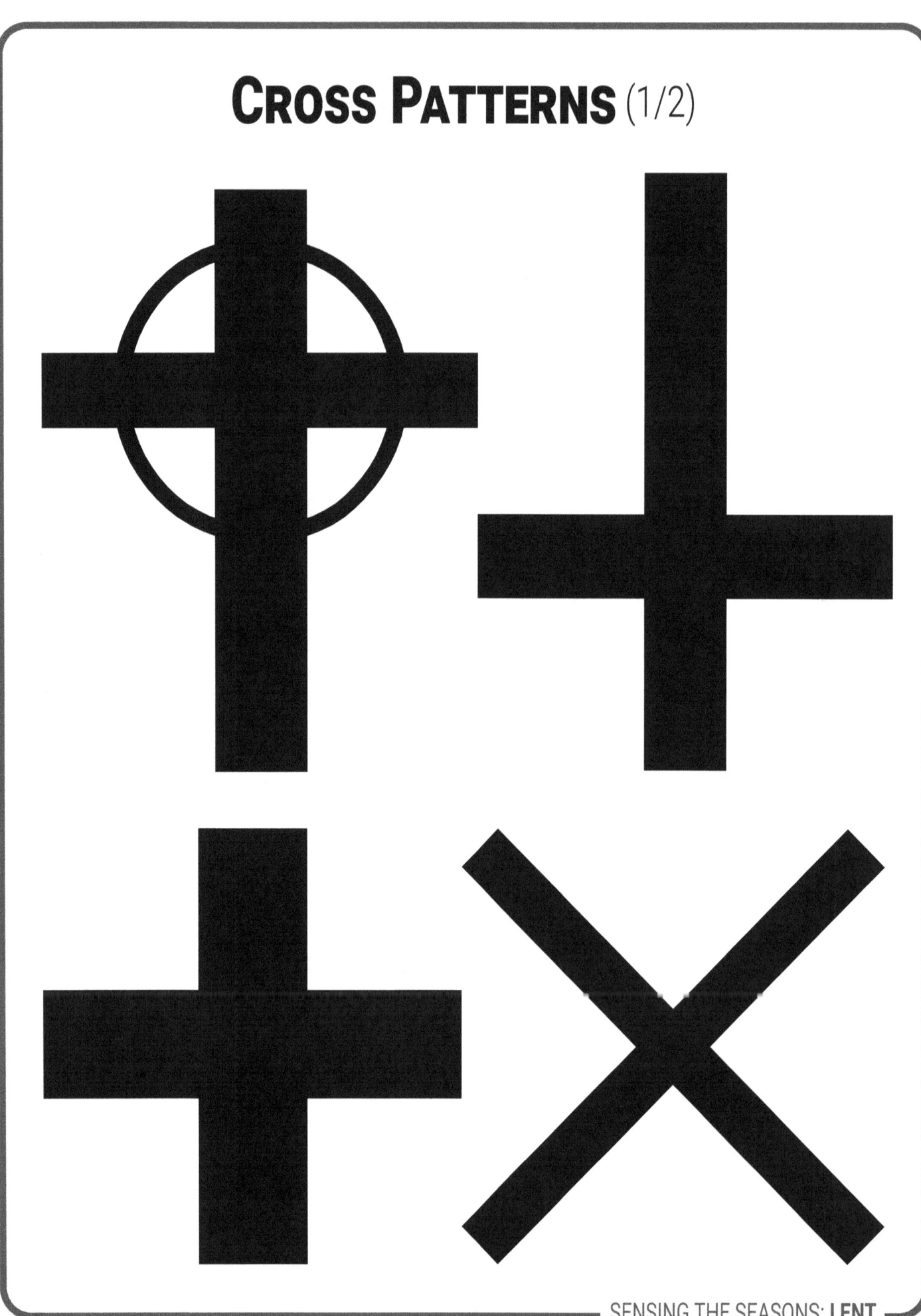

SENSING LENT

Scented Soap Balls

Materials

- Bars of soap, white—1 to 1½ per participant
- Bowls
- Cheese cloth or muslin
- Cups (optional)
- Herbs, fresh aromatic such as lavender, mint, sage, rosemary, thyme
- Kettle or electric tea pot
- Knives (optional)
- Markers
- Measuring spoons
- Paper, construction
- Peelers for vegetables
- Pens
- Pitcher
- Scissors
- Strainers
- String
- Water

Advance Preparation

- Boil water, fill a pitcher, and set in learning center.

Method

Some Lenten observances have been borrowed from Passover traditions. Thorough house cleaning during this springtime holiday has a religious significance for Jewish families. While the period of Lent for Christians may also be a time of physical cleaning, it is a time of spiritual house cleaning too. In the season of Lent, make scented soap balls to use or to give as gifts during this period of "cleansing."

Select a bowl, bars of soap, and a knife or vegetable peeler. Cut up one and one-half bars of white soap by chopping them into small slivers or shaving with a vegetable peeler. Place the soap pieces in the bowl. In a separate bowl, or a large cup, measure one teaspoon of an aromatic herb such as lavender, mint, rosemary, sage, or thyme. Carefully measure and pour ¾ cup boiling water over the herbs. Allow the mixture to steep for a few minutes. Strain out herbs and pour the hot water over the cut up soap. Use hands to mix well until soap chips are moist, but not soupy. Set aside for about 15 minutes or until mixture is mushy.

While waiting for the soap mixture to set, prepare gift tags. Cut construction paper to desired size. Use markers and pens to decorate the cards and print a message for the recipient.

Cut three 8-inch pieces of cheesecloth or muslin. In addition, cut three 12-inch pieces of string. Set both aside to use for the soap balls.

Use hands to mix softened soap again and divide into three parts. Place each portion on a square of cheesecloth or muslin and form it into a ball shape. Pull cloth tightly around each soap ball, gather at the top, and tie firmly with string.

Take soap balls home and hang them in a warm place to dry for about three days or until soap is completely hard. Remove fabric wrapping. Place soap in a basket or a dish and enjoy using it. Or, wrap each ball, add a tag, and give them as gifts.

SENSING LENT

Prayer Poems

Materials

- Bibles
- Copy machine or printer
- Paper
- Pens
- Resource sheet: Prayer Poems

Advance Preparation

- Duplicate the resource sheet.

Method

Writing activities, especially poetry, can help people discover creative ways to "find their voice" and express their thoughts and feelings. During the season of Lent, especially the special days of Ash Wednesday, the Sundays of Lent, Palm Sunday, Holy Thursday (also called Maundy Thursday), Good Friday, and Holy Saturday, meditations can be enhanced by using creative writing.

Experiment with a variety of poetry patterns as a way to reflect, remember, and respond to the events that took place throughout Jesus' ministry and in the last weeks, and days, of Jesus' life.

Use a copy of the Prayer Poems resource sheet as a guide. Review the variety of poetry patterns, and the topics related to Holy Week, and compose verses on the suggested subjects. In addition, look through a Bible to find other passages and themes that would be meaningful for the writing project. Once the prayer poems are completed, use them during personal devotions throughout the season of Lent.

Prayer Poems (1/2)

Day and Story/Theme	Type/Pattern	Example
Ash Wednesday Jesus cleanses the temple	Rhyme - 4 lines ▶ Lines 2 and 4 rhyme	Jesus cleansed the temple and called it a house of prayer. On Ash Wednesday we cleanse our hearts so Jesus is welcome there.
Sundays in Lent Jesus' teachings	Quick couplet - 2 lines ▶ 3 syllables in each line	Jesus' words Must be heard - Let me live to forgive!
Palm Sunday Jesus' triumphal entry	Cinquain - 5 lines ▶ Line 1 - 1 word noun ▶ Line 2 - 2 adjectives that describe the noun ▶ Line 3 - 3 "ing" words that describe the noun ▶ Line 4 - 4 words that express a feeling about the noun ▶ Line 5 - 1 word that is a synonym for the noun	Jesus Divine, human Loving, sharing, giving A friend of mine Savior

SENSING THE SEASONS: LENT

Prayer Poems (2/2)

Day and Story/Theme	Type/Pattern	Example
Holy Thursday — Jesus' betrayal	Diamond – 5 lines ▶ Line 1 - 1 word that is an opposite of line 5 ▶ Line 2 - 2 words which describe line 1 ▶ Line 3 - 3 words which resolve the conflict ▶ Line 4 - 2 words which describe line 5 ▶ Line 5 - 1 word which is an opposite of line 1	Betrayal Deception; Dishonesty Conscience; Sincerity; Trust Faithful; Steadfast Loyalty
Good Friday — Jesus' crucifixion	Free Verse ▶ A pattern without rhyme and meter	On the Friday called "good," we experience God's gift of love.
Holy Saturday — Jesus' death	Acrostic ▶ Print theme word vertically down left side of paper. Write one word associated with theme for each letter.	Q - Quiet our fears U - Unite our spirits I - Inspire our thoughts E - Energize our hearts T - Touch our lives OR use letter of acrostic as first letter of word, for example: Q-uiet our fears ...
Easter Sunday — Jesus' resurrection (butterfly)	Shape poem ▶ Shape of theme	*(butterfly shape poem: "New life through Jesus' resurrection.")*

SENSING THE SEASONS: LENT

SENSING LENT

Lenten Foods Concentration Game

Materials

- Clips, binder or paper type
- Copy machine or printer
- Dishes and serving utensils for food examples
- Envelopes, manila (Optional)
- Foods, or packages or pictures, associated with concentration game including:
  - Chocolate eggs or jelly beans
  - Hot Cross Buns
  - Macaroni and cheese
  - Pancakes
  - Pretzels twists
  - Soup
  - Unleavened bread
  - Water
- Forks (optional)
- Markers or pens
- Napkins (optional)
- Paper, cardstock for game and bond for take home sheet
- Plates (optional)
- Resource sheets:
  - Concentration Game Cards
- Tape (optional)

Advance Preparation

- Assemble Lenten food examples—either packages, pictures, or samples.
- Copy several sets of the Concentration Game Cards on full sheets of cardstock. Pages are provided with an optional pattern for the backs of the cards. Clip each set together or place in a labeled manila envelope. Duplicate extra copies of the card resource sheets for families to take home.

Method

Fat Tuesday, Fastnachts, and Fasting are a few of the special days, foods and traditions associated with the season of Lent. Throughout the centuries, symbolic foods have played an important part in helping Christians observe the time from Ash Wednesday through Holy Saturday. Learn more about the customs associated with this 40 day period by playing a game of concentration.

While a game of concentration usually includes pairs of identical pictures to be matched, each set in this Lenten version has one card with the name of a special day, such as Good Friday, and information about the food connected with it. The second, or matching card, has a picture of the food, in this case, hot cross buns.

Begin by selecting a set of playing cards. Read the name of each important day of Lent, information about the food connected with it, and view a picture of the item.

If examples of the foods connected with the game are provided, take a plate, napkin, and fork and sample them. If there are boxes, packages, or pictures of the foods, take time to look at each of them.

After the review, shuffle the cards. Lay out the set, picture side down, in a tiled pattern in the center or on a floor or table. As an alternative, tape them to a wall. The goal is to turn the cards, one at a time, and attempt to match each day of Lent with its respective food. Turn over two cards. If they match, remove them from the playing pieces. If they do not match, replace them and turn over two more cards. Play continues until all pairs have been uncovered.

When the game is over, take resource sheets home and make a game for teaching others about the traditions of the special days of Lent. The cards could also be turned into a book to share with family and friends.

CONCENTRATION GAME CARDS (1/4)

Shrove Tuesday

Pancakes: Also called Mardi Gras, Fat Tuesday, or Carnival, this is considered the last day to feast before the fast of Lent begins on Ash Wednesday. Pancakes are the traditional food because they use up rich ingredients and are fried in fat. Donuts called Fastnachts or Pazcki are sometimes eaten as well.

Ash Wednesday

Fasting/Water: The traditional beginning of Lent, this day initiates 40 days of preparation for celebrating the Resurrection on Easter Sunday. Fasting, or going without food or just drinking water for a specific period of time, is an outward sign of penitence and repentance and a personal discipline to discern God's will.

Lent

Pretzels were made by Roman monks in the 5th century and distributed to the poor on certain days before Easter. Because the dough, made from only flour, salt, and water, was twisted to represent arms crossed in prayer, pretzels became symbols to remind people of the holiness of the season.

Fridays in Lent

Macaroni and Cheese, Vegetable Soup, Fish: Throughout the season of Lent, simple meals—especially those that are meatless—are emphasized. Fish sticks, macaroni and cheese or hearty soups might be the main dish for dinner on a Friday during Lent.

Palm Sunday

Dates: Since dates grow on palm trees, and the crowd waved palm branches and spread them on the ground as Jesus entered Jerusalem on Palm Sunday, dates are a symbolic treat for the first day of Holy Week.

Holy Thursday

Unleavened Bread: During the Old Testament Passover (Exodus 12), the Israelites had to flee Egypt in such a hurry they did not have time for the bread to rise. When Jesus and the disciples observed the Passover in the upper room on Holy Thursday (Maundy Thursday), they would have eaten unleavened bread.

Good Friday

Hot Cross Buns are baked with raisins inside and shiny brown tops on the outside. They are marked with a cross of white icing as a reminder of the significance of the day on which Jesus was crucified.

Holy Saturday

Baskets: On this day baskets are prepared with special foods to eat on Easter Sunday. These treats often include colored eggs, representing new life, chocolates, and a cake in the shape of a lamb, representing the lamb that was slain as a sacrifice for sin.

Concentration Game Cards (2/4)

SENSING THE SEASONS: LENT

Concentration Game Cards (3/4)

SENSING THE SEASONS: LENT

Concentration Game Cards (4/4)

SENSING THE SEASONS: LENT

SENSING LENT
Educational Eggs

Materials

- Bibles
- Copy machine or printer
- Egg cartons—1 per person
- Eggs, plastic—12 per person
- Glue
- Markers, permanent
- Markers, washable
- Paper, construction
- Paper for printer
- Resource sheet: Educational Eggs
- Scissors

Advance Preparation

- Purchase one dozen plastic eggs per participant.
- Decide if the items for the eggs will be actual objects, images, or symbols created on felt. Suggestions for actual items, which can be found in craft, hobby, party, and teacher stores—especially in a charm, miniature, or sticker section—include:

  1. Palm branch—piece of emerald palm leaf from a florist or from a silk plant
  2. Coin(s)—silver coin(s)
  3. Bread or cup—mini plastic loaf of bread or small plastic communion cup
  4. Praying hands—sticker of praying hands
  5. Whip—narrow strip of leather
  6. Cross
  7. Crown of Thorns—piece of branch with thorns
  8. Nail
  9. Dice—one die
  10. Linen—strip of linen fabric
  11. Stone
  12. Empty—leave egg empty

- Duplicate the resource sheets.

Method

Just like a calendar might be used during Advent to count the days to Christmas, a carton of plastic eggs with story symbols can become a tool used to share the events that led to Jesus' crucifixion and resurrection. Prepare a set of educational eggs to review the stories and to teach them to others, especially during Holy Week.

Select an empty egg carton. Pick twelve plastic eggs. Print a number on each egg—beginning with 1 and ending with 12. Place the prepared eggs in the carton for storage.

Pick up a copy of the chart listing the events, scripture passages, and symbols connected with each part of the story. Cut the strips apart; they will be put into the respective eggs along with each object.

Begin with the first egg, number one. Select the strip of paper associated with it. Review the title of the specific event that took place in the life of Jesus. Look up and read the scripture passage associated with it. Make or select the item connected with the story. For example, for Jesus' Triumphal Entry—egg one—read Matthew 21:8-9. Fold the paper to fit into the egg. Select the palm branch symbol, or pick a piece of paper with the illustration(s), or draw and cut it from felt. Place the paper and the symbol inside the first egg and set it back in the carton. Repeat the procedure for the remaining 11 eggs.

After the eggs are filled and the set is prepared, decorate the top of the carton by cutting and gluing a piece of construction paper to the lid, using markers to create a design and a title, and adding a name.

Use the set of eggs to review the stories of Holy Week, to share them with others, and to celebrate that the last egg is empty because the tomb was empty on Easter morning. Rejoice in the risen Savior's gift of eternal life.

Option

There are many additional events and stories from the last week of Jesus' life that could be used for the individual eggs. Feel free to make substitutions if desired.

EDUCATIONAL EGGS

Egg	Event	Scripture	Symbol
1	Jesus' Triumphal Entry	Matthew 21:8-9	Palm Branch
2	Jesus' Betrayal	Matthew 26:14-15	Coin(s)
3	Jesus' Passover Meal	Matthew 26:26-28	Bread or Cup
4	Jesus' Prayer	Matthew 26:39	Praying Hands
5	Jesus Whipped	Matthew 27:26	Leather Strip
6	Jesus' Carries His Cross	John 19:17	Cross
7	Jesus' Crown of Thorns	Matthew 27:29	Crown of Thorns
8	Jesus Nailed to the Cross	Matthew 27:35	Nail
9	Jesus' Garments Divided	Matthew 27:35	Dice
10	Jesus' Burial	Matthew 27:59	Linen
11	Jesus Sealed in a Tomb	Matthew 27:60	Stone
12	Jesus' Resurrection	Matthew 28:6	Empty Egg

SENSING THE SEASONS: LENT

Sensing Easter

John 11:25-26

> *Jesus said to her, 'I am the resurrection and the life. Those who believe in me, even though they die, will live, and everyone who lives and believes in me will never die. Do you believe this?'*

The season of Easter begins with Easter Sunday and celebrates the resurrection. The date of Easter changes each year based on the cycles of the moon. Easter Sunday is the first Sunday after the first full moon on or after March 21 (the approximate vernal equinox). So Easter can be as early as March 22 or as late as April 25. Some scholars say the day for Easter was set to assure the light of the moon for pilgrims traveling to Jerusalem. Obviously, the first Easter followed the Jewish celebration of the Passover. The Orthodox churches continue to use Passover as the determining date for Easter services with their Palm Sunday occurring the first Sunday after Passover begins.

On the first Easter morning, God made a difference for human beings forever. God raised Jesus from death to new life. Easter is a season of hope that invites God's people to rejoice that because Jesus lives, we, too, will live—eternally. Easter reminds us that we can experience God's renewal now and forever when we believe in Christ's resurrection.

Easter is more than a special day in the church year. It is actually a season of 50 days in which we celebrate the joy of the new life Christ's resurrection brings to the world. But even more, as we proclaim God's plan of hope and salvation for all people, we discover that Easter is a way of life. During the season of Easter, or Eastertide as some call it, Christians celebrate the Resurrection and tell the stories of Jesus' appearances to the disciples. Ascension Day occurs during this season, 40 days after Easter Sunday, and celebrates Jesus' return to heaven to reign at the right hand of God. The promise of the gift of the Spirit and the challenge to "go into all the world" are a part of the Easter season as well.

The color for Easter is white, the color reserved for the holiest festivals of the church year.

SENSING EASTER

Butterfly Banners

Materials

- Copy machine or printer
- Glue, tacky or tape
- Markers—bold, pastel, and "day-glo" colors
- Needles for sewing (optional)
- Paper, cardstock for butterfly patterns
- Pins, straight
- Pipe cleaners
- Resource sheet: Pattern for Banner Butterflies
- Ribbon, wide white or yellow
- Rods, small brass or large embroidery hoops
- Scissors
- Thread (optional)

Advance Preparation

- Duplicate the resource sheet on cardstock paper for each participant.

Method

Add to the pageantry of Easter by making a ribbon banner adorned with butterflies.

Select a sheet of butterflies and use a variety of markers of various colors to decorate them. Cut out the shapes.

Finish the brightly colored butterflies with pipe cleaner antennae. Fasten a pipe cleaner to the middle of the body with tacky glue or small bits of tape. Fold along the middle so the wings stand up on each side of the pipe cleaner.

Decide whether to make a circle banner using an embroidery hoop or an arrangement on a brass curtain rod. Cut ribbons into one to two foot lengths or, for a different look, vary ribbon lengths. Glue or stitch the top of each ribbon over the hoop or rod. Trim the bottom of each strip into points.

Pin butterflies along the ribbons—some in perched positions with wings up and some in an almost flat pose.

To use the creation, hang the banner where a breeze will move the ribbons and cause the butterflies to flutter.

Option

This could easily become a project involving many people if each made butterflies and contributed them to one large circle or rod.

Pattern for Banner Butterflies

SENSING EASTER

Egg Decorations

Materials

- Balloons
- Clothes line (optional)
- Containers for glue mixture or starch
- Flowers or leaves, artificial
- Glue, tacky or glue guns and sticks
- Glue, white or liquid starch
- Oils for flower scents
- Paper, waxed
- Ribbon, narrow
- Scissors
- Thread, embroidery cotton or thin string
- Water

Advance Preparation

- Create a mixture of ⅔ white glue and 1/3 water and pour into a few containers.
- As an addition, or alternative, pour liquid starch into several containers, too.

Method

Experience several sensory sensations by forming an airy, delicate Easter egg decoration.

Blow up a balloon into an egg shape—about six to eight inches.

Cut a length of cotton embroidery thread or thin string at least 18 inches long. Saturate the thread or string in the glue or starch mixture. Pull the thread between first and second fingers to scrape off excess glue. Carefully wrap string around the balloon, criss-crossing threads. Continue until there is a strong netting covering the balloon.

Allow the balloon to dry on waxed paper in a warm place. If there is a clothesline available, eggs may be tied to the line to dry.

When the thread is completely dry, pop the balloon with a scissor blade. Remove the balloon through one of the larger openings.

Trim the remaining "egg" with bunches of artificial spring flowers which have been dabbed with essential oils to simulate the smells of the season. Cluster the flowers as well as ribbons at the top of the egg. Tie on a loop of ribbon to form a hanger.

The eggs will be firm to the touch and cage-like. Use several eggs to make a mobile, hang as tree decorations, or arrange in a basket.

Flower Pot Bells

Materials

- Beads or buttons, large
- Bells, large jingle type
- Brushes for paint
- Clean up supplies
- Cord
- Flower pots, tiny terra cotta (with holes drilled in the bottom)
- Paint, acrylic
- Rag or towel
- Vinegar
- Water

Advance Preparation

- Wash the terra cotta flower pots with a towel dipped into a mild vinegar and water solution. This will clear away any dust or mineral deposits on the clay surface. Allow the pot to dry before painting it.

Method

There are many Lent and Easter legends connected with bells. In France, no bells or chimes ring from Good Friday until Easter morning. In Italy, people say the bells fly away to Rome for the season of Lent. When the bells return on Easter Sunday, they drop colored eggs for children to find. Happy occasions, such as Easter, are often announced by the ringing of bells. Easter music frequently features the bright sounds of bells and trumpets.

Design a flower pot bell to help ring in the season of Easter. Select a small terra cotta pot for the project.

Use acrylic craft paints and tiny brushes to decorate the flower pot. Designs may include Christian symbols and spring flowers. Be sure to paint the pot upside-down, not right-side-up.

Thread two ends of cord or twine through the hole in a large bead or through the holes in a large button. Tie a knot at the bottom of the bead or button—allowing the ends of the cord to extend beyond the knot.

Tie a jingle bell onto the remaining cord. Pull the loop up through the flower pot hole to form a hanger for the bell. The bead or button and knot will allow the jingle bell to hang freely for a better sound.

Give the bell as a lovely symbol of Easter and tell others about the legends of the bells.

SENSING EASTER

Butterfly Shaped Snacks

Materials

- Ingredients and supplies for snack
- Knives
- Napkins
- Plates
- Toaster (optional)

Method

Easter celebrations bring to mind traditional foods: spring lamb or baked ham, asparagus, hard boiled eggs, holiday breads, and jelly beans.

Create new traditions by featuring a favorite Easter symbol, the butterfly, as a special snack for the season. Cut bread—toast, if possible—diagonally and place on a plate with triangles joined to resemble a butterfly. For a morning snack, spread with strawberry or pineapple cream cheese. Add an orange section and slivers of orange peel for body and antennae. For a lunch time treat, spread bread or toast with colorful vegetable cream cheese. Use a baby carrot for the body and green pepper strips for antennae. As an alternative, cut the bread with butterfly shaped cookie cutters.

In addition, sample butterfly shaped snacks such as cookies, crackers, and gummies.

Option

If a meal is involved use large "bow tie" pasta called farfalle—which means butterfly—for salad, soup, or casseroles.

Block Print Cards

Materials

- Bowls, containers, or plastic lids for paint
- Copy machine or printer
- Cotton or polyfil
- Knife, craft or utility
- Paint, acrylic—variety of colors
- Paper, card stock for printer
- Paper, construction
- Paper, scrap
- Plastic wrap, roll
- Pencils
- Resource sheet: Pattern for Butterfly Blocks
- Scissors
- String, twist-ties, or yarn
- Styrofoam blocks/sheets, 4" x 6"
- Water

Advance Preparation

- Duplicate several copies of the butterfly pattern onto card stock paper and cut out the shapes.
- Place a butterfly pattern on top of a Styrofoam block and trace around the shape. Using a craft knife, cut into the Styrofoam along the pattern line to a depth of ¼ inch. Cut the Styrofoam around the outside of the design to a depth of ¼ inch. The butterfly design should be higher than the background. Prepare at least one block for every color of paint.
- Pour each paint color into a small bowl, container, or plastic lid.
- Make dabbers for transferring paint to the Styrofoam block. For each, roll a piece of cotton or polyfil into a small ball shape. Place it in the center of a square of clear plastic wrap. Bring the sides up around the cotton and tie the wrap with a string, twist-tie, or yarn. Slightly flatten the bottom. Make one dabber for each color of paint and set it next to the corresponding container.

Method

Block printing is a technique in which a raised design formed on a base is dipped into paint and pressed onto paper. Beautiful Easter cards can be created from this process.

Pick a sheet of construction paper. Fold it in half to form a card.

Select a Styrofoam block with a butterfly design. Decide on the color of paint to use for the project. Pick a dabber, a tool used to apply paint to the Styrofoam block. Dip the dabber into the selected paint color with a quick up and down motion. Transfer the paint to the Styrofoam block with the same dapping motion. On scrap paper, turn the block over and press the design onto it. Repeat several times until the results are satisfactory and the technique is mastered. If the paint is too thin, add more. If it is too thick, add additional water. Create the design on the card.

When the paint is dry, or even before the process is started, write an Easter greeting on the inside of the card.

If there is time, and supplies are available, make additional cards. Take the cards home and give them to family and friends.

Option

For easier preparation, use rubber stamps and ink pads to create the cards.

SENSING THE SEASONS ■ LEARNING CENTERS FOR THE CHURCH YEAR

Pattern for Butterfly Blocks

Sensing Pentecost

John 14:15-17

> *'If you love me, you will keep my commandments. And I will ask the Father, and he will give you another Advocate, to be with you forever. This is the Spirit of truth, whom the world cannot receive, because it neither sees him nor knows him. You know him, because he abides with you, and he will be in you.'*

Fifty days after Easter at the Jewish harvest festival of Pentecost, God sent the gift of the Holy Spirit. The Spirit's coming was marked by a mighty wind that moved the disciples from the upper room out into the marketplace, as well as by tongues of flame that danced above them and infused them with power to share the story of Jesus in whatever language the listening crowd could understand. A third symbol of Pentecost became the descending dove representing baptism and the quiet presence of the Spirit. Pentecost was the birthday of the church when Peter preached the first sermon and the first converts were made. The Sunday after Pentecost is often celebrated as Trinity Sunday, the recognition that God's revelation is now complete as God the Creator, or Father; God the Redeemer, or Son; and God the Empowering Presence, or Holy Spirit.

For congregations that celebrate Pentecost as a season rather than a day, it begins 50 days after Easter Sunday and continues until the day before the First Sunday of Advent.

Pentecost is a long period that focuses on the importance of the Christian mission. Lessons include Jesus' teachings to the disciples, especially challenges to be in mission and to share God's love. "What does it mean to be a Christian?" and "What does it mean to be the Church?" are questions appropriate for the time of Pentecost.

The color for Pentecost is red for the fire of enthusiasm and the force of energy that God's empowerment brings.

SENSING PENTECOST

Trinity Triptych

Materials

- Copy machine or printer
- Glue
- Markers
- Paper, construction or poster board—12" x 18"
- Paper for printer
- Paper, gold foil wrap (optional)
- Pencils
- Resource sheet: Symbols for the Trinity
- Scissors
- Trims like braid, cording, rick rack (optional)

Advance Preparation

- Duplicate the resource sheets for each participant.

Method

With the coming of the Holy Spirit on Pentecost, Christians believe God revealed the Trinity, or three-in-one concept of God: God as Father or Creator of life, God as Jesus or Redeemer of life, and God as Spirit or Sustainer of life. Of course, this does not mean we worship three gods. The Trinity is a mystery we accept by faith and understand by experience.

To illustrate the concept of the Trinity, make a triptych, or three fold display, that is an ancient Christian art form. A triptych was often used to feature three pictures or images about God, Jesus, and the Holy Spirit and to remind people of the Trinity. Each picture or image would be displayed in a separate arched panel, yet the three panels were connected.

Refer to the resource sheet with ideas and symbols to illustrate the concept of the Trinity. They include: apple, cube, fleur-de-lis or iris, person, pottery, shamrock, triangle, and water. Then pick an image to use in the design of a triptych celebrating the Holy Spirit.

Construct the triptych. Fold twelve-inch by eighteen-inch construction paper or poster board into thirds across the width. Use a pencil to draw simple arches at the top of each panel. All three sections can be the same size or the center panel can be left taller.

Choose a symbol, or symbols, to depict on the triptych. Separate one symbol into its parts to highlight on the different panels or use a separate symbol on each section of the artwork. Whichever plan is selected, draw the symbols on each panel or cut them from construction paper and glue them in place.

Add colored foil paper for a background or trim the edges with braid, cord, or rick-rack to add an elegant touch to the triptych.

Once the design is complete, stand the triptych as a table decoration. Be sure to explain the meaning behind the symbol(s) chosen to represent the Trinity.

Symbols for the Trinity

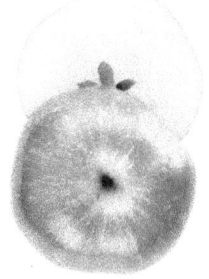

Apple

An apple has three parts—the outer layer or skin, the sweet fruit, and the inner core containing the seeds—yet it is one piece of fruit.

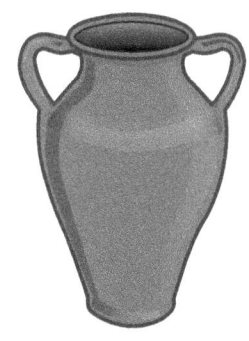

Pottery

A clay pot is an "earthen vessel" like human beings, a trinity created by the potter's skilled hands, the wet clay, and the power of the turning wheel.

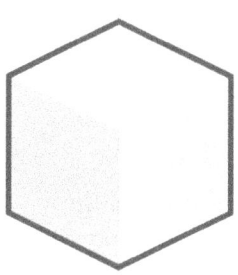

Cube

A cube is three dimensional containing height, and width, and depth.

Shamrock

Legend says that St. Patrick explained the Trinity by using the three-leafed shamrock of Ireland, pointing out that it was one plant with one stem yet it had three separate leaves.

Fleur-de-lis or Iris

This symbol from French royalty has three flower petals, yet is one flower. An iris has the same symbolism.

Triangle

While it is one distinct shape, a triangle is made of three sides.

Person

A person can be thought of as a father/mother, as a son/daughter, or as a brother/sister, yet he or she is still the same person.

Water

Water is two parts hydrogen and one part oxygen, yet the same chemical substance can be experienced in its liquid form or as a solid—ice, or as a vapor—steam.

SENSING THE SEASONS: PENTECOST

SENSING PENTECOST
Guided Meditation

Materials

- Copy machine or printer
- Paper
- Pencils or pens
- Resource sheets:
  - Guided Meditation for Pentecost
  - Pentecost Sentence Starters

Advance Preparation

- Duplicate copies of the Guided Meditation for Pentecost resource sheet for the learning center.
- Make a copy of the Pentecost Sentence Starters resource sheet for each participant.

Method

Often people tend to think of the events of Pentecost in limited ways. Some think theologically about how God poured the Holy Spirit upon the Church. Many concentrate on the tongues of flame and the apostles' speaking in tongues. The story that Luke tells in Acts 2, however, is rich in sensory references. Use a Guided Meditation as a way to heighten the senses of sight, smell, sound, taste, and touch while reflecting on the story of Pentecost in a new way.

Read the Guided Meditation for Pentecost script silently or aloud, in a reflective, thoughtful manner.

Take time to think about the experience. Consider questions like:

- What did you learn?
- What new things did you discover about Pentecost?
- How did the meditation highlight the senses ... sight, smell, sound, taste, and touch?

As a conclusion to the activity, take one of the Pentecost Sentence Starters sheets and a pencil or pen. Write responses to the phrases on the sheet:

- Pentecost is the sound of ...
- Pentecost is the sight of ...
- Pentecost is the taste of ...
- Pentecost is the smell of ...
- Pentecost is the touch of ...

If others are at the learning center, share reflections, if desired.

Pentecost Guided Meditation

Imagine the apostles gathered together in one place for the Festival of Pentecost. You are there with them. It is the day of this special feast. People have arrived from near and far. Yours is just one of the groups which have gathered. Who is in your group? You have come to be with these people at this time.

You are together in a house large enough that everyone can sit together in one room. The apostles are talking together about Jesus. Perhaps you can hear some of them talking about the Resurrection, or the way Jesus appeared to them. You are eating together. What foods are you eating? Maybe there are some of your own favorite foods that are a part of the feast. Perhaps your mouth begins to water as you smell the wonderful offerings.

Suddenly you hear a loud wind. It is almost deafening—like the sound of a tornado. The sound is so loud you may see dishes shake and hear them rattle. You feel the building vibrate from the sound. As you look at each other in surprise and fear, you see what looks like fire in the middle of the room. As you watch, the fire breaks up into pieces which look like little tongues. They come and land on the head of each person in the room.

Although the "tongues" look like fire, you don't feel any heat or burning. The temperature in the room doesn't change. Instead, something else begins to happen. People start to discover that suddenly they can speak in languages they have not studied. Everyone knows it is a special gift from the Lord. What does it sound like as everyone in the room discovers this new gift? You all decide to go out and use this special gift to tell all the strangers in town about Jesus' resurrection.

As you start to leave the house, you see that strangers have come to find out what the loud noise was coming from your house. They must have thought there was some sort of disaster. You can tell that these are travelers from the look and smell of their clothes, as well as their accents. You see confused looks on their faces when they hear the apostles speaking foreign languages. People in the crowd are mumbling to one another as they try to figure out what is going on. Someone tries to explain the languages by saying that you are all drunk.

When Peter hears this, he uses it as an opportunity to tell everyone about Jesus. You listen as he tells about the resurrection and how prophecies are being fulfilled. He speaks powerfully, and you can see that many people are interested by the way they pay attention to what he is telling them.

Someone asks what they must do to be saved and Peter tells them to repent and be baptized. Now many people say, "I want to be baptized, too." You and the apostles go to the nearest body of water to baptize all these people. When you get there, you all go down into the water together. You feel the coolness of the water as you enter it. You participate in the baptism of hundreds of people. When you finish, you are wet and very tired, but you all sing a song of praise together in thanks to God for what God has done.

SENSING THE SEASONS: PENTECOST

Pentecost Sentence Starters

Pentecost is the sound of . . .

Pentecost is the sight of . . .

Pentecost is the taste of . . .

Pentecost is the smell of . . .

Pentecost is the touch of . . .

SENSING PENTECOST

Bottle Puppets

Materials

- Bible
- Bottles, dishwashing or laundry detergent
- Fabric scraps
- Felt
- Glue
- Scissors
- Tape, duct
- Trims
- Tubes, cardboard—various sizes
- Yarn or fake fur

Advance Preparation

- Clean the bottles and remove their labels.

Method

After Jesus ascended to heaven, his friends returned to the upper room where they had celebrated the Passover and the Lord's Supper. Confused and scared, they were not sure what to do next. Jesus had promised the disciples that he would send them a special gift. Suddenly, as they waited together, there came a sound like a mighty rushing wind. Tongues of fire landed on their heads and people began to speak in different languages. Filled with the Holy Spirit, Jesus' followers went into the city. On Pentecost, Peter preached a sermon about the wonderful things that Jesus had done. When Peter invited believers to repent and be baptized, over 3,000 people joined the church.

Make and use puppets from recycled paper tubes and plastic bottles to tell the story of Pentecost to others.

Read the story of Pentecost in the Bible, Acts 2. Decide which character(s) to make. It could be Peter or another disciple. It might be one of the women who followed Jesus or a boy, girl, man, or woman in the crowd.

Pick a bottle. Turn it up-side-down and decide if the side with the handle will form the front of the face or the back. If it is to be the front, the handle becomes the puppet's nose. Place a paper towel tube on the pouring spout of the bottle. It will become the rod by which the puppet is operated. Use duct tape to secure the two pieces together.

Form the face by cutting eyes and a mouth from felt scraps. Glue them in place. Eyebrows, eyelashes, and cheeks may be added.

Make hair from yarn, fake fur, or polyfil. Glue it to the top of the puppet head.

Choose a large square of fabric for the costume. Cut a small hole in the center of the material and slide the paper tube through it. Tape the fabric to the neck of the puppet. Add contrasting pieces of cloth, as well as trims, to complete the costume.

When the puppet is complete, have the character share his or her eyewitness account of the events of Pentecost. Be sure to have the person describe and include the sounds that took place as well. If other people are at the learning center, work together to share the story.

Option

If the class or group participating in the learning center activities gathers at the end of the session, they could join together to act out the story of Pentecost as the scripture passage is read by a narrator.

SENSING PENTECOST

Meringues

Materials

For preparing meringues:

- Bowl
- Cookie sheets
- Ingredients for meringues (see recipe)
- Measuring cups and spoons
- Mixer
- Oven
- Paper grocery bags, brown
- Pencils
- Recipe for meringues (provided)
- Scissors
- Spoon

For serving meringues

- Bowls or plates
- Candle lighter or matches (optional)
- Candles, small birthday (optional)
- Forks or spoons
- Fruit such as cut up peaches and strawberries
- Ice cream
- Scoop for ice cream
- Whipped cream

Advance Preparation

- Since meringues take an hour to bake and often an additional hour to harden, they may be prepared in advance. If they are baked before the session, place each shell on a separate plate and set the desserts in the learning center along with the toppings.

Recipe for Meringues

- Ingredients:
- 3 egg whites
- 1 teaspoon vanilla
- 1/4 teaspoon cream of tartar
- 1 cup sugar
- Dash of salt

Instructions:

- Cover a baking sheet, or more than one, with a single layer of brown paper bag cut to fit the pan. Draw six circles, about four inches in diameter, as a guide for the shell size.
- Put egg whites in a bowl and bring them to room temperature. Add cream of tartar, a dash of salt, and vanilla. Beat to soft peaks. Very gradually add sugar, mixing until stiff peaks form and sugar is completely dissolved. Meringue will be glossy.
- Spread one-third cup meringue on each circle on the brown paper on the cookie sheet. Use the back of a spoon to shape the mixture into a meringue shell shape which is a hollowed out center with sides.
- Bake the shells at 275 degrees F for one hour. For crisper meringues, turn off the heat and allow shells to dry in oven (door closed) for an additional hour.

Method

Capture the spirit of the day of Pentecost, especially the memory of the wind, by eating an airy confection called a meringue. Since meringues take an hour to bake, and sometimes an additional hour to harden, the shells were made in advance. Now they are ready to be filled with goodies and enjoyed as a special treat.

Select a plate with a meringue on it. Choose any or all of the toppings provided—cut up fruit, ice cream, whipped cream—and fill the cavity of the shell with these treats.

Since some churches celebrate Pentecost as the birthday of the church and honor the day with a traditional birthday party, add a tiny candle to the dessert. Carefully light the candle.

Pick a fork or a spoon and enjoy the delicious delicacy.

Option

If the meringues will be baked during the session, begin the process at the beginning of the gathering so they can be ready to fill and eat at the conclusion.

SENSING PENTECOST
Dove Mobiles

Materials

- Copy machine or printer
- Feathers, white
- Glue
- Paper lace doilies
- Paper, white cardstock
- Pens or pencils
- Resource sheet: Pattern for Doves
- Sandpaper
- Scissors
- Skewers, wooden
- Tape
- Thread

Advance Preparation

- Duplicate copies of the dove pattern on white cardstock paper.

Method

In the Bible, a white dove is one of the symbols representing the Holy Spirit. Although the word dove is not specifically mentioned in the Acts 2 account of Pentecost, there is a reference to the Holy Spirit descending on those present. Gospel passages also describe the descending dove at the baptism of Jesus: Matthew 3:16-17, Luke 3:21-22, and John 1:32-34.

In celebration of Pentecost and as a reminder that the Holy Spirit is present in the hearts and lives of every believer, create a unique mobile with doves and feathers.

Using the cardstock patterns provided, trace and cut out four paper doves.

As an alternative to using the pattern, a simple white dove can be created from the shape of a hand. Trace carefully around a hand extending the thumb so it becomes the dove's head and the closed fingers form the tail feathers. Cut out the dove and add details with pen or pencil. Bits of paper lace, from white doilies, can be glued on for trim.

Use the pointed end of a skewer to pierce a small hole in the top of each shape. Slide thread though the holes and secure with knots.

Select two skewers to be the horizontal bars for the mobile. Cut or break off the pointed tip of both skewers and smooth the ends with sand paper. Tie a dove near each end of the two bars.

Form an "x" or a plus—"+"—sign with the two skewers and latch them together with thread. To prevent the lashing threads from sliding, put a drop of glue at the spot where the two sticks are bound together. Tie a thread from the center of the joined bars to use as the hanger.

Glue several feathers to each dove to add a soft texture and a feathery feeling. Allow the mobile to swing freely to determine if all of the doves are balanced. If not, merely slide the ties along the horizontal bars until the doves are fairly steady.

To enjoy the mobile, hang it in a place where a gentle breeze will cause the doves to move.

PATTERN FOR DOVES

SENSING THE SEASONS: **PENTECOST**

Sensing Ordinary Time

Matthew 28:18-20

And Jesus came and said to them, 'All authority in heaven and on earth has been given to me. Go therefore and make disciples of all nations, baptizing them in the name of the Father and of the Son and of the Holy Spirit, and teaching them to obey everything that I have commanded you. And remember, I am with you always, to the end of the age.'

One divergence in the church year occurs with the celebration of Ordinary Time. It is important to note that this term does not mean common or mundane. Rather, it comes from the word "ordinal" which is simply means "counted" time. Catholics observe Ordinary Time following the Christmas/Epiphany celebrations until the beginning of Lent and again from the First Sunday after Pentecost to the start of Advent. After Pentecost, the First Sunday is called Trinity Sunday and the last is known as Christ the King, or Reign of Christ, Sunday.

Some other churches divide the long summer and fall of Pentecost into an early and late time in the same season. Others celebrate a Trinity Time that focuses on the completeness of God's revelation. Still others refer to it as Growing Time or Kingdomtide to serve as an interim from the push of Pentecost and the preparation of Advent.

Ordinary Time is the longest period in the church's calendar with 33 or 34 Sundays and weeks. Ordinary Time is a season of discipleship and growth. Lessons focus on following in Christ's footsteps and becoming who God hopes we will be. Individual involvement and responsibility are challenges of Ordinary Time. Personal growth and spiritual nurture should lead to outreach and ministry, with disciples who offer both the name of Jesus and the cup of cold water. The season of Ordinary Time lasts until four Sundays before Christmas, when the new church year begins again with Advent.

The color for Ordinary Time is green, the color for growth.

SENSING ORDINARY TIME
Wire Fish Pendants

Materials

- Cardboard or tablet backs
- Cutters for wire
- Felt, dark colors
- Glue, craft or tacky
- Glue gun and glue sticks (optional)
- Hole punch
- Illustration of Christian fish symbol:
- Needles, large
- Ribbon or yarn
- Scissors
- Scissors, pinking shears (optional)
- Thread, dark colors
- Wire, brass and copper—fine and heavy

Advance Preparation

- Cut felt into 4" circles. If possible, use a pinking shears on the edges to give a finished look.
- Cut cardboard circles a little smaller than the felt. Pink the edges, if desired.
- Snip heavy wire into 8" lengths.
- Cut yarn into 30" pieces.

Method

In Bible times, fishing was an important industry. In fact, at least four of the people Jesus called to be the first disciples were involved in this trade—Andrew, James, John, and Peter. In Matthew 4:19 Jesus tells his followers to leave their nets to become "fishers of people." In the early church, when the first letters—ΙΧΘΥΣ (ichthys)—of five Greek words were combined, the arcs formed the shape of a fish. Also, the letters formed an acrostic with the English translation "Jesus Christ, God's Son, Savior." During times of persecution, the fish symbol, with its important message, became a way for Christians to identify each other and know it was safe to share the Gospel.

Throughout the world, the simple fish emblem is still used to communicate with other believers. Make fish symbol pendants to wear as a sign of personal faith.

Choose one cardboard and two felt circles. Stack the felt, cardboard, then felt, and glue each layer. Use a punch or a darning needle to make a hole near the top of the pendant. Thread ribbon or yarn through the hole and tie the ends.

Look at the pictures of the simple fish emblem used by early Christians. Using the heavy wire, form the figure by bending the length in half. Curve the wire on each side to give the fish fullness, then cross over the tail portion of the fish. Twist a small strand of fine wire around the "X" where the pieces cross. For a more intricate fish, wrap a long piece of fine wire around the "crossed" tail and continue wrapping along the entire outline. Additional wire can be twisted on, if needed.

Fasten the wire fish form to the felt backing by sewing the "front and tail" with fine wire. An optional means of fastening would be to use tiny drops of hot glue on each end of the fish.

Wear the fish symbol as a pendant during Ordinary Time—a season of discipleship—or anytime to proclaim the message to others of being a follower of Jesus.

SENSING ORDINARY TIME
Herb Bottles and Gardens

Materials

For Scent Bottles

- Bibles
- Bottles, small, from pills, spices, or travel size containers—7 per person
- Containers for extracts, oils, or spices (if not in original cans or jars)
- Copy machine or printer
- Cotton balls—7 per person
- Cotton swabs or eye droppers
- Extracts, oils, or spices:
  - Aloe
  - Cinnamon or saffron
  - Cummin, dill, or mint
  - Frankincense or myrrh
  - Lavender
  - Mustard, dry
  - Thyme
- Markers, permanent
- Paper for printer
- Resource sheet: Seasons, Spices, Scripture
- Scissors

For Herb Gardens

- Containers for seeds such as peat pots or small cups or tubs
- Craft sticks
- Markers, permanent
- Scoops, shovels, or spoons
- Seeds for dill, mint, and mustard
- Soil for potting
- Spray bottles
- Water

Advance Preparation

- Duplicate resource sheet.

Method

Ordinary Time, the longest segment of the church calendar, is to be anything but common or mundane. In fact, the name for this time in the cycle comes from the word "ordinal," which simply means "counted" time. Throughout these weeks, often 33 or 34 Sundays of Ordinary Time, the focus is on faith formation, growth as Jesus' disciples, and the proclamation of the Gospel to those near and far.

Since Ordinary Time emphasizes growth as Christians, take time to learn about—and to grow—a variety of plants mentioned in the Bible.

Aloe, dill, saffron. Cinnamon, mint, thyme. Cummin, hyssop, mustard. All are herbs, plants, or spices, and all are mentioned in the Bible. In fact, through the years, each of these seasonings has been connected with a specific time in the church calendar.

Learn about the season, the spice, and the scripture, and make sensory sniff bottles to use as a guessing game with friends or to give as a gift to a family with children.

Select a copy of the resource sheet to learn more about the seasons, the spices, and the scripture. Then gather seven of each—empty bottles, cotton balls, and cotton swabs. Use a permanent marker to print the name of each season on a separate bottle. For each period in the church calendar, beginning with Advent, read the information on the sheet: season, spice, scripture. Then cut the strip for that period off of the sheet. Fold or roll the paper to fit inside the bottle labeled Advent. Locate the container with the lavender. Use a cotton swab to transfer a few drops or a small amount of the spice to a cotton ball. Place the scented ball in the labeled container. Repeat the process until the seven bottles are filled.

Take the set of scent bottles home and play a guessing game with others to see if they can identify the scent, or give them as a gift to a family with children.

Next, start a family herb garden and grow several of the plants mentioned on the Season, Scent, Scripture list and used in the set of sniff bottles.

If three different types of seeds are provided—for example, dill, mint, and mustard—pick three containers. Print the family name on the outside of each pot. Next, scoop or spoon soil into a carton until it is near the top, about ¾ full. Pick two or three seeds for the first type of plant, for example dill. Place them in one hand and carefully use the fingers of the other hand to gently push the seeds into the top of the soil. Scoop a small amount of additional soil on top of the seeds. Use a spray bottle to squirt the soil with water, like a gentle rain. Pick a craft stick, and a permanent marker, and print the name of the herb on the marker. Insert the stick into the pot. Repeat the process for the remaining herbs. Take the herb garden home, place the containers in a window sill so the plants receive light, and water them each day.

SEASONS, SPICES, SCRIPTURE

Season	Herb/Spice	Scripture
Advent	Lavender - Meditation and reflection	Luke 2:19 - But Mary treasured all these words and pondered them in her heart.
Christmas	Thyme - Herb used as food for animals	Luke 2:7 - And she gave birth to her firstborn son and wrapped him in bands of cloth, and laid him in a manger, because there was no place for them in the inn.
Epiphany	Frankincense, Myrrh - Spices given to Christ Child as gifts from Magi	Matthew 2:11 - On entering the house, they saw the child with Mary his mother; and they knelt down and paid him homage. Then, opening their treasure chests, they offered him gifts of gold, frankincense, and myrrh.
Lent	Cummin, Dill, Mint - Jesus' teachings	Matthew 23:23 - 'Woe to you, scribes and Pharisees, hypocrites! For you tithe mint, dill, and cumin, and have neglected the weightier matters of the law: justice and mercy and faith. It is these you ought to have practiced without neglecting the others.'
Easter	Aloe - When entering the empty tomb, the disciples would have smelled the spices in the linens used to embalm Jesus' body	John 19:39-40 - Nicodemus, who had at first come to Jesus by night, also came, bringing a mixture of myrrh and aloes, weighing about a hundred pounds. They took the body of Jesus and wrapped it with the spices in linen cloths, according to the burial custom of the Jews.
Pentecost	Cinnamon, Saffron - Pungent, red spices associated with the excitement of Pentecost	Acts 2:42 - They devoted themselves to the apostles' teaching and fellowship, to the breaking of bread and the prayers. Solomon 4:14 - Nard and saffron, calamus and cinnamon, with all trees of frankincense, myrrh and aloes, with all chief spices
Ordinary Time	Mustard - Small seed that grows to large plant	Matthew 13:31 - He put before them another parable: 'The kingdom of heaven is like a mustard seed that someone took and sowed in his field;'

SENSING THE SEASONS: ORDINARY TIME

SENSING ORDINARY TIME
Rhythm Instruments

Materials

Materials for specific instruments:

- Cymbals
  - Compact discs, used—2 per project
  - Fabric strips, 12"—2 per project
- Flutes
  - Straws, plastic—various colors—8 per project
  - Tape—cellophane, duct, or masking
- Guitars
  - Box with open tops—1 per project
  - Rubber bands, various widths—4-6 per project depending on size of box
- Maracas
  - Egg, plastic—1 per project
  - Pebbles
  - Spoons, plastic—2 per project
  - Tape, masking
- Mandolins
  - Embroidery hoops, 2 parts—1 per project
  - Rubber bands—6 per project
- Pin Strummer
  - Bobby pins
  - Foam or Styrofoam block or thick sponge
  - Tape (optional)
- Scissors

Advance Preparation

- Decide which instruments to construct and assemble the materials for them. If necessary, delete the directions from the instructions before printing them for any instruments that will not be made.

Method

Ordinary Time coincides with the season of summer on the secular calendar. Summer often includes school break, family vacations, and camp sessions. Many of these seasonal activities celebrate the wonders of God's creation—camping under the stars, enjoying a beautiful beach, and hiking through the woods. These and other nature experiences stimulate the senses in many ways—the sight of stars covering the sky, the smell of pines in a forest, the sound of water in a babbling brook, the feel of pebbles smoothed by sand, and the taste of a ripe peach picked from a tree.

As a way to praise God for the beauty of creation, make a variety of rhythm instruments from natural or recycled items.

Decide which instruments to make and follow the directions for one or more activities.

Cymbals

Select two CDs, compact discs, and two strips of fabric. Loop a strip of fabric through the hole of each CD. Tie off the material at a point where the fabric strap will slide snugly around three or four fingers of the hand. While these cymbals do not make a resounding crash, they do produce a fun clack.

Flutes

Arrange eight straws, the same or different colors, in a line. Cut one end of each to varying lengths, with the longest straws on the left side and the shortest straws on the right. Wrap tape—clear cellophane, patterned duct, or colored masking—around the row of straws. The tape should be tight enough to hold the pieces together but loose enough so the straws do not bunch up.

Blow through the straws to make sounds. Enjoy the variety of pitches caused by the differing lengths of the pieces.

Guitars

Pick a rectangle-shaped cardboard box with an open top or a tissue box with a hole in the center. Select large rubber bands, of various widths, and stretch several elastic pieces around the box. Bands of various widths will ensure that the guitar strings produce different sounds and tones when plucked.

Maracas

Fill a plastic egg with small pebbles. Position the inside concave portions of two plastic spoons across from each other on two sides of the egg. Wrap tape around the bowls of the spoons to secure them tightly to the egg. Secure the bottom of the spoon handles with tape as well. Shake to play.

Mandolins

Choose an embroidery hoop and separate the two pieces. Stretch four to six rubber bands across the inner circle of the hoop. Nest, or place, the inner hoop into the outer one, being careful not to jostle the rubber bands. If there is a screw, tighten it.

Pin Strummers

Pick a block of foam or Styrofoam or a thick sponge to use as the base of the strummer. Select six bobby pins, or a number that can be spaced out at one-fourth to one-half inch intervals, across the base. Widen or gently open the bobby pins. Insert one end of each pin into the foam or sponge. Allow the other end of the bobby pin to hang above the base. To play, gently push down on the pin's end and allow it to pop back up.

To achieve different sounds, vary the base material. If a small cardboard box or a little metal container is used, run a strip of tape across the bottom side of a row of bobby pins. Strum the pins to play the instrument.

Once the instruments are constructed, use them in private as well as public devotions involving dance and music.

Option

If there is a closing activity for the event, include a song where musicians can play their rhythm instruments.

SENSING ORDINARY TIME

Memorizing Bible Verses

Materials

- Bibles
- Chalk boards, white boards, or magic slates—small individual size
- Chalk for chalk boards, dry erase markers for white boards, or styluses for magic slates
- Markers
- Paper
- Pencils or pens

Method

During the season of Ordinary Time, Christians focus on being followers of Jesus day after day. One of the ways believers develop as disciples is by committing favorite Bible verses to memory. Scripture helps us savor the lessons of faith, or as Psalm 34:8 reminds us: "Taste and see that the Lord is good." If we memorize small bites of the Word of God, then we can have a "taste" of what it means to be a follower of Jesus all the time. Many children, youth, and adults choose to memorize Psalm 23 as a statement of faith that helps them remember the goodness of God. Try these two ways to commit the Shepherd's Psalm to memory.

Say the Missing Words

- Locate Psalm 23 in a Bible.
- Write the verses of Psalm 23 on a chalk board, white board, or a magic slate.
- Read the words of the Psalm out loud.
- Repeat each portion—phrase or verse—of the Psalm out loud several times.
- Erase key words, but keep reading the verses, supplying the missing words.
- Keep erasing more words until the complete passage can be recited without anything written at all.

Make a Rebus

Create a rebus puzzle, or story, for Psalm 23. A rebus is a type of game or riddle composed of pictures and symbols, as well as letters. For example, instead of writing the word "I" an illustration of an "eye" would be used in its place.

Select a Bible, a piece of paper, and a marker, pen, or pencil. Print the first line, or verse, of Psalm 23 as a rebus. For example: The Lord is my [shepherd]. Instead of writing the word shepherd, put a picture of one in that space.

Continue writing out the Psalm, substituting pictures whenever possible. Repeat the same picture every time a word is used.

Post the rebus version of the Shepherd's Psalm and "read" it often. The pictures will help the words come to mind.

Use these and any other helpful methods until the 23rd Psalm is committed to memory. Once the passage, is memorized, savor the words as part of daily devotions, or disciplines, during the season of Ordinary Time.

SENSING ORDINARY TIME

Flowering Branches

Materials

- Branches, bare
- Containers for tissue paper
- Glue
- Hole punch
- Markers
- Paper, construction
- Paper, tissue—green plus colors for seasons such as:
  - Spring—pastel shades of lavender, pink, yellow
  - Summer—vivid hues of orange, purple, red
  - Fall—vibrant colors of gold, orange, red
  - Winter—subtle tones of blue, gray, white
- Pens
- Pictures of branches with blossoms (optional)
- Ribbon, string, or thread
- Scissors

Advance Preparation

- Collect bare branches that are not too large or too thick.
- Cut tissue paper into one inch squares. Place pieces in a container or separate each color into a separate basket, box, or tub.

Method

Just like there are seasons of the calendar year such as summer and winter, there are also seasons of the church year, like Christmas and Easter. In the church year, Ordinary Time occurs when Christians are not preparing for or celebrating Advent, Christmas, Epiphany, Lent, Easter, or Pentecost. Ordinary Time generally occurs twice in the liturgical cycle—first, after Christmas and Epiphany until the beginning of Lent, and, second, after Easter and Pentecost until the beginning of Advent. During Ordinary Time believers are challenged to develop as disciples and to share God's love in their daily lives. Since Ordinary Time is a period of growth, create a unique branch as a reminder to grow during this season and all seasons—calendar year and church year.

Begin by decorating the branch. Look at pictures of flowering bushes, shrubs, and trees and simulate this effect on a limb to represent the growth expressed in all seasons. Plan the placement of the tissue paper blossoms. Pastel shades of pink, lavender, and yellow for spring; vivid hues of green for summer; vibrant colors of gold, orange, and red for fall; and subtle tones of blue, gray, and white for winter could be scattered across the entire branch or placed in separate sections of the limb. Regardless of the arrangement, liberally sprinkle shades of green throughout to represent the color of Ordinary Time.

Once the plan is determined, create the blossoms. Select the colors of tissue paper to use. Dot each piece of tissue with glue in the center, and then press it onto the branch. Continue until the branch is bright with flowers.

Next, make a list of ways to grow as a Christian—every day but especially during the church season of Ordinary Time. Take a piece of paper and a pen or a pencil and list at least seven ways—one for every day of the week—or 12—one for each month of the year—ideas which might include:

- Give to causes that do God's work
- Meet with other Christians for fellowship and fun
- Partake of the sacraments
- Pray
- Read the Bible
- Serve in Jesus' name
- Study biblical topics such as justice or peace
- Use talents in God's service
- Worship

For each way to grow, cut a random design or a shape—circle, rectangle, square—from poster board. Cards should be proportionate to the size of the branch. To make a commitment for each day of the week, cut seven cards, or prepare twelve tags if there is a goal for each month. Use a marker or a pen to print an item from the list on each card. Poke or punch a hole at the top of each shape. Use ribbon, string, or thread to form a loop through each hole. Attach the cards to the branch as a reminder of ways to grow during each season.

Enjoy the blossoms by placing the branch on a dresser as a reminder of personal growth each day or ask permission to set it on a table to share the message with family and friends.

Resources

Age Group Suggestions

Learning doesn't occur in a simple, straightforward way. Learning is a layering process that happens over time. Lessons may be visited and revisited, with slightly different emphases and tasks, teaching the same story, but in a different way and on a different level. Adapting content to various age groups is a challenge, but with some practice an educator can remodel any lesson plan to fit the needs of a given group of learners.

There are a few basic rules to keep in mind when adjusting plans to fit age groups:

- Determine any prior knowledge that students may already know or need to know in order to participate.
- Begin with what is known and familiar and build a bridge to new ideas and concepts.
- Move from concrete to abstract concepts.
- Use a variety of approaches that incorporate different multiple intelligences.

For example, the goal to teach the story of the church year would need to be adapted depending upon the age of those involved in the lesson. Using the guidelines suggested above, that goal could be met whether planning for preschoolers or seniors in high school. Children absorb the importance of the seasonal celebrations that are a natural part of our culture. Therefore, they will easily understand and respond to the story of faith as it unfolds through the seasons of the church year. Adapt lessons to teach the colors, names, stories, symbols, and meanings used to communicate the universal message of faith. As the patterns become familiar, they will connect the rhythm of the year with the recurring themes of hope and love that are at the heart of each season.

Preschool: Colors

- Emphasize the colors of each of the seasons of the church year.
- Drape a table in the room with the appropriate color for each season. Let the children help change the colors when needed.
- Make a paper plate calendar and color it to represent each season of the church year.
- Take a walk through the church each time the colors change.

Early Elementary (K-2)—Names and Order

- Emphasize the names of the seasons and their order in the cycle.
- Create or purchase a church year calendar and point out the progression from one season to the next.
- Make a puzzle with colors and names of the seasons for children to sequence.
- Sing the names of the seasons to the first phrases of the tune, "Twinkle, Twinkle, Little Star." In the second phrase of the first line of the song, double time the notes on the words "Easter" and "Pentecost" and again for "God's love."

> Advent, Christmas, Epiphany,
> Lent, Easter, Pentecost
> tell God's love for me.

Upper Elementary (3-5)—Stories

- Emphasize the stores of faith that are celebrated with each season.
- Create a video box and let children draw the Bible stories that reflect the season's message on a roll of paper.
- Divide into groups, one for each season, and act out the Bible stories appropriate for each cycle.
- Have each child write an explanation of how their family celebrates one or all of the seasons.

Middle School (6-8)—Symbols

- Emphasize the symbols of the season.
- Create a bulletin board to display the symbols and the season each represents.
- Draw the symbols or create collages for original bulletin cover artwork.
- Play a concentration game using the names and the symbols for the seasons.

High School (9-12)—Meaning

- Emphasize the meaning behind each season.
- Choose hymns to sing or read and discuss how their words relate the message of the season.
- Map out the progression of the story of faith as it unfolds through the seasons; then write or share aloud a corresponding map of personal faith, for example—Just born? Just baptized? Suffering? Renewed? In mission?
- Write original prayers to be used during each season.

CATHOLIC CHURCH YEAR OVERVIEW (1/2)

Season/Feast	Date(s)	Theme(s)	Color(s)
Church Year	1st Sunday of Advent through Christ the King Sunday, the last Sunday of Ordinary Time	**Remember** – God's love	Combination of colors for specific days/seasons
Advent	Four Sundays before Christmas Day through Christmas Eve	**Review** – God's promise of the Messiah	Violet (Pink/Rose for joy on 3rd Sunday)
Christmas Season	From sunset Christmas Eve (December 24) through the Sunday after Epiphany	**Rejoice** – Jesus, the Savior's, birth	White, Gold
Epiphany	January 6 (or observed on a Sunday between January 2-8)	**Reveal** – Jesus, Redeemer of the world	White, Gold
Ordinary Time (Winter)	Between Christmas Season and Lent, ending on Mardi Gras/Fat Tuesday	**Respond** – Christians grow in discipleship	Green
Ash Wednesday	The 1st day of Lent: the Wednesday seven weeks before Easter	**Repent** – Christians repent	Purple
Lent	From Ash Wednesday through Holy Thursday, with 40 days of fasting (not counting Sundays)	**Reflect** – Jesus' ministry	Purple
Holy Week	The Week before Easter, including Palm Sunday, Holy Thursday, and Good Friday	**Reflect** – Jesus' suffering	Red
Palm Sunday	The Sunday beginning Holy Week	**Reflect** – Jesus as King	Red

SENSING THE SEASONS: THE CHURCH YEAR

Catholic Church Year Overview (2/2)

Season/Feast	Date(s)	Theme(s)	Color(s)
Holy Thursday	The Thursday before Easter	Reflect – Jesus' institutes the Lord's Supper	White
Good Friday	The Friday before Easter	Reflect – Jesus' death	Red
Easter Sunday	The Sunday after the first full moon after March 21	Renew – Jesus' resurrection	White
Easter Season	Seven weeks after Easter, including Ascension	Renew – Jesus' appearances	White
Pentecost	The 7th Sunday after Easter	Receive – Holy Spirit empowers believers	Red
Ordinary Time (Summer/Fall)	The day after Pentecost to the day before Advent	Respond – Jesus' followers in mission	Green
Trinity Sunday	The Sunday after Pentecost	Respond – Christians affirm the Triune God	White
Christ the King Sunday	The last Sunday before Advent	Respond – Christians confirm Christ as present and future king	White

Ecumenical Church Year Overview (1/2)

Season/Feast	Date(s)	Theme(s)	Color(s)
Church Year	1st Sunday of Advent through Christ the King Sunday, the last Sunday of Ordinary Time	**Remember** – God's love	Combination of colors for specific days/seasons
Advent	Four Sundays before Christmas Day through Christmas Eve	**Review** – God's promise of the Messiah	Violet, sometimes blue (Pink for joy on 3rd Sunday)
Christmas Season/Christmastide	12 Days from sunset December 24 through January 5	**Rejoice** – Jesus, the Savior's, birth	White, Gold
Epiphany	January 6	**Reveal** – Jesus, Redeemer of the world	White, Gold
Ordinary Time (Winter) or Epiphany season	Between Christmas Season and Lent, ending on Shrove/Fat Tuesday	**Respond** – Christians grow in discipleship	Green
Ash Wednesday	The 1st day of Lent: the Wednesday seven weeks before Easter	**Repent** – Christians repent	Black or Gray, Purple
Lent	The 40 weekdays before Easter, not counting Sundays, including Holy Week	**Reflect** – Jesus' ministry	Purple
Holy Week	The Week before Easter, including Palm Sunday, Maundy/Holy Thursday, and Good Friday	**Reflect** – Jesus' suffering	Red
Palm Sunday	The Sunday beginning Holy Week	**Reflect** – Jesus as King	Red, Gold, Purple, White

SENSING THE SEASONS: THE CHURCH YEAR

Ecumenical Church Year Overview (2/2)

Season/Feast	Date(s)	Theme(s)	Color(s)
Maundy/Holy Thursday	The Thursday before Easter	Reflect - Jesus' institutes the Lord's Supper	Red
Good Friday	The Friday before Easter	Reflect - Jesus' death	Black
Easter Sunday	The Sunday after the first full moon after the vernal equinox	Renew - Jesus' resurrection	White, Gold
Eastertide/ Easter Season	Seven weeks after Easter, including Ascension	Renew - Jesus' appearances	White, Gold, Red
Pentecost	The 7th Sunday after Easter	Receive - Holy Spirit empowers believers	Red
Ordinary Time (Summer/Fall)	The day after Pentecost to the day before Advent	Respond - Jesus' followers in mission	Green
Trinity Sunday	The Sunday after Pentecost	Respond - Christians affirm the Triune God	White, Gold
Christ the King Sunday	The last Sunday before Advent	Respond - Christians confirm Christ as present and future king	White, Gold

SENSING THE SEASONS: THE CHURCH YEAR

Church Year Themes (1/2)

Season/Feast	Emphasis	Message
Advent	Preparation and waiting for the coming of Christ in Bethlehem, in our hearts, and at the end of history.	We examine and prepare our hearts that we may be renewed in repentance, patience, and anticipation to welcome the coming of Christ.
Christmas	The prophecies are fulfilled: the Messiah is born. The Savior of the world has arrived.	We express our joy, give thanks to God, and embrace God's presence in Jesus Christ.
Epiphany	The manifestation of Jesus as the Savior to the Jews and to the whole world.	We celebrate Jesus as the light of God and the manifestation of God to the world.
Ordinary Time (Winter)	The manifestation of Christ as the Son of God.	We grow with a new commitment to manifest the life of Christ through our own witness.
Lent	Time to travel with Christ through his suffering and preparation for death; time for prayer, meditation, fasting, and almsgiving.	We examine ourselves, repent of our sins, and renew our dedication to Christ through our identification with the journey of Jesus to the cross.
The Great Triduum (Holy/Maundy Thursday, Good Friday, Holy Saturday)	Remembrance of the institution of the Lord's Supper, the washing of the disciples' feet (Holy Thursday), and the trial and crucifixion of Christ (Good Friday),	We use these "three great days" as a time of fasting and prayer; reflection on the suffering and death of Jesus; and a commitment to live in the pattern of his death and resurrection.
Easter Sunday	The most crucial event of the Christian year! A celebration of the great saving event of the resurrection of Jesus for the victory over sin and death.	We celebrate Jesus' victory as the culmination of salvation history and are called to the Christian life of dying to sin and rising to the life of the Spirit.

SENSING THE SEASONS: THE CHURCH YEAR

Church Year Themes (2/2)

Season/Feast	Emphasis	Message
Eastertide/ Easter Season	The continued ministry of Jesus gives credence to his resurrection and ascension and is a time to reflect on his reign as the sovereign Lord who intercedes for us in the presence of God, the Father.	We reflect on the implications of Jesus' resurrection and ascension, commit ourselves to live as those who are "risen with Christ," living under his reign.
Pentecost	The powerful outpouring of the Holy Spirit on the church for witness and service.	We are called to walk with the Spirit and participate in the growth and spread of the Christian church in the world.
Ordinary Time (Summer/Fall)	The Church of Christ enters the world with the Gospel of Christ and the presence of the Holy Spirit to witness to God's saving love.	We embrace the teachings of the church, grow deeper into the truths of God's saving events in history, and grow in discipleship and service.

Adapted from *Ancient-Future Time - Forming Spirituality through the Christian Year* by Robert E. Webber (Grand Rapids, MI: Baker Books, 2004).

Methods Index

Art

Beaded Pins	The Church Year	Touch	28
Block Print Cards	Easter	Touch	77
Clock Face Calendars	The Church Year	Sight	16
Cross Symbols	Lent	Sight	54
Decorated Candles	Advent	Sight	34
Dove Mobiles	Pentecost	Touch	88
Educational Eggs	Lent	Touch	70
Egg Decorations	Easter	Smell	74
Evergreen Prints	Christmas	Touch	46
Flower Pot Bells	Easter	Sound	75
Flowering Branches	Ordinary Time	Touch	99
Herb Bottles and Gardens	Ordinary Time	Smell	93
Incense Holders	Epiphany	Smell	49
Lavender Sachets	Advent	Smell	35
Memorizing Bible Verses	Ordinary Time	Taste	98
Mini Wreaths	Advent	Touch	39
Music Mobiles	Advent	Sound	36
Rhythm Instruments	Ordinary Time	Sound	96
Sand Painted Cards	Epiphany	Sight	48
Scented Soap Balls	Lent	Smell	58
Shell Covered Chests	Epiphany	Touch	52
Stained Glass Ornaments	Christmas	Sight	42
Trinity Triptych	Pentecost	Sight	80
Wire Fish Pendants	Ordinary Time	Sight	92

Banners/Textiles

Butterfly Banners	Easter	Sight	72
Colorful Weavings	The Church Year	Smell	19
Mini Jingle Bell Wreaths	Christmas	Sound	44

Creative Writing

Block Print Cards	Easter	Touch	77
Bottle Scale Songs	The Church Year	Sound	21
Flowering Branches	Ordinary Time	Touch	99
Guided Meditation	Pentecost	Smell	82
Prayer Poems	Lent	Sound	59
Sand Painted Cards	Epiphany	Sight	48

Culinary

Butterfly Shaped Snacks	Easter	Taste	76
Colorful Weavings	The Church Year	Smell	19
Cookie Gifts	Advent	Taste	37
Crisp Rice Star Treats	Epiphany	Taste	51
Gingerbread with Topping/Sauce	Christmas	Taste	45
Herb Bottles and Gardens	Ordinary Time	Smell	93
Meringues	Pentecost	Taste	86
Pomander Balls	Christmas	Smell	43
Snack Sacks	The Church Year	Taste	24

Drama

Bottle Puppets	Pentecost	Sound	85
Sound Effects	Epiphany	Sound	50

Games

Educational Eggs	Lent	Touch	70
Herb Bottles and Gardens	Ordinary Time	Smell	93
Lenten Foods Concentration Game	Lent	Taste	62
Snack Sacks	The Church Year	Taste	24

Music

Bottle Scale Songs	The Church Year	Sound	21
Music Mobiles	Advent	Sound	36
Rhythm Instruments	Ordinary Time	Sound	96

Photography

Lenten Foods Concentration Game	Lent	Taste	62

Puppetry

Bottle Puppets	Pentecost	Sound	85

Storytelling

Educational Eggs	Lent	Touch	70
Guided Meditation	Pentecost	Sound	82
Memorizing Bible Verses	Ordinary Time	Taste	98
Sound Effects	Epiphany	Sound	50

Scripture Index

Old Testament

Exodus 12:8	Smell	Ordinary Time	93
Exodus 13:1-10	Introduction	The Church Year	7
Deuteronomy 6:1-9	Introduction	The Church Year	7
Psalm 22:27-31	Overview	The Church Year	15
Psalm 23	Taste	Ordinary Time	98
Psalm 34:8	Taste	Ordinary Time	98
Song of Solomon 4:14	Smell	Ordinary Time	93
Isaiah 9:6-7	Overview	Christmas	41
Isaiah 11:1-3a	Overview	Advent	33

New Testament

Matthew 1	Overview	Christmas	41
Matthew 2	Overview	Christmas	41
Matthew 2:1-12	Sound	Epiphany	50
Matthew 2:1-2, 7, 9-10	Taste	Epiphany	51
Matthew 2:11	Smell	Ordinary Time	93
Matthew 2:11	Overview	Epiphany	47
Matthew 2:11	Touch	Epiphany	52
Matthew 3:16-17	Touch	Pentecost	88
Matthew 4:19	Sight	Ordinary Time	92
Matthew 13:31	Smell	Ordinary Time	93
Matthew 21:8-9	Touch	Lent	70
Matthew 23:23	Smell	Ordinary Time	93
Matthew 26:14-15	Touch	Lent	70
Matthew 26:26-28	Touch	Lent	70
Matthew 26:39	Touch	Lent	70
Matthew 27:26	Touch	Lent	70
Matthew 27:29	Touch	Lent	70
Matthew 27:35	Touch	Lent	70

Reference	Section	Season	Page
Matthew 27:59	Touch	Lent	70
Matthew 27:60	Touch	Lent	70
Matthew 28:6	Touch	Lent	70
Matthew 28:18-20	Overview	Ordinary Time	10
Luke 1	Overview	Christmas	41
Luke 2	Overview	Christmas	41
Luke 2:7	Smell	Ordinary Time	93
Luke 3:21-22	Touch	Pentecost	88
Luke 22:19-20	Introduction	The Church Year	7
John 1:1-14	Overview	Christmas	41
John 1:32-34	Touch	Pentecost	88
John 3:16	Introduction	The Church Year	7
John 3:16	Overview	Lent	53
John 11:25-26	Overview	Easter	71
John 14:15-17	Overview	Pentecost	79
John 19:17	Touch	Lent	70
John 19:39-40	Smell	Ordinary Time	93
Acts 2	Smell	Pentecost	82
Acts 2	Sound	Pentecost	85
Acts 2	Touch	Pentecost	88
Acts 2:1-4	Introduction	The Church Year	7
Romans 6	Introduction	The Church Year	7
Philippians 2:8-11	Introduction	The Church Year	7
1 Timothy 3:15	Introduction	The Church Year	7
Titus 2:13-14	Introduction	The Church Year	7

About the Authors

Anna L. Liechty

Anna Liechty taught English to high school students and served as adjunct faculty for Indiana University South Bend for many years. Anna also worked as a mentor trainer and teacher coach with adult learners for the Indiana Department of Education. She won numerous educational classroom grants, including the Eli Lilly Teacher Creativity grant.

As a life-long church educator, Anna worked with all age levels, directing Sunday morning and youth programming, consulting with congregations about their educational ministry, and writing a wide variety of religious education materials. She served as Vice President of Active Learning Associates and co-authored four Lilly Worship Renewal grants.

Anna's undergraduate degree is from Bowling Green State University in Ohio and her Master's degree from Indiana University South Bend. She was certified by the National Board for Professional Teaching Standards in Adolescent and Young Adult English Language Arts.

In retirement, Anna continues to pursue a variety of writing projects, receiving an Individual Artist Grant in Literature from the Indiana Arts Commission. Now living in Florida, Anna enjoys traveling with her husband Page Foster, a retired pastor, and counting the days between visits with six children, twelve grandchildren, and seven great-grandchildren.

Phyllis Vos Wezeman

As a religious educator, Phyllis Wezeman has served as Director of Christian Nurture at a downtown congregation in South Bend, Indiana; Executive Director of the Parish Resource Center of Michiana; and Program Coordinator for ecumenical as well as interfaith organizations in Indiana and Michigan.

In academics, Phyllis has been Adjunct Faculty in the Education Department at Indiana University South Bend and in the Department of Theology at the University of Notre Dame. She is an "Honorary Professor" of the Saint Petersburg (Russia) State University of Pedagogical Art where she has taught methods courses for extended periods on several occasions. She has also been guest lecturer at the Shanghai Teachers College in China.

As founder of the not-for-profit Malawi Matters, Inc., she develops and directs HIV & AIDS Education programs with thousands of volunteers in 200 villages and more than 1,500 schools in Malawi, Africa including "Creative Methods of HIV & AIDS Education," "Culture & HIV-AIDS," and "Equipping Women/Empowering Girls."

Author or co-author of over 2,000 articles and books, she has written for over 80 publishers.

Phyllis served as President of Active Learning Associates, Inc.; a consultant or board member to numerous local and national organizations such as the American Bible Society, Church World Service, LOGOS, and the Peace Child Foundation; leader of a six-week youth exchange program to Russia and Ukraine; and Project Director for four Lilley Worship Renewal grants. She is the recipient of three "Distinguished Alumni Awards," the Aggiornamento Award from the Catholic Library Association, and the 2021 Lifetime Achievement Award from the Association of Presbyterian Church Educators (APCE).

Wezeman holds undergraduate degrees in Business, Communications, and General Studies from various institutions and an MS in Education from Indiana University South Bend.

Phyllis and her husband Ken (who met when they were in second and third grade in elementary school) have three children and their spouses, Stephanie (Jeff), David, and Paul (Deha); five grandchildren, Quin, Ayle, Lief, Ashley, and Jacob; and two great-grandsons, Maddox and Troy.

MORE ENGAGING RESOURCES BY phyllis vos wezeman

- DOWNLOADABLE
- REPRODUCIBLE
- SHARABLE
- AFFORDABLE

Seeing Jesus
Social Justice Activities for Today Based on Matthew 25

60 creative, interactive learning activities for all ages based on the parable of the last judgment: "Lord, when was it that we saw you hungry... thirsty... a stranger... naked...sick or in prison...?"

224 PAGES • 8½"x 11"

DOWNLOADABLE WITH OPTIONAL PAPERBACK

52 Interactive Bible Stories

A Collection of Action, Echo, Rhythm, and Syllable Stories

Participants will love these playful ways of expressing Scripture.

74 PAGES • 8½"x 11"

DOWNLOADABLE WITH OPTIONAL PAPERBACK

100 Creative Techniques for Teaching Bible Stories

A treasure chest of fun ideas and activities, split across ten categories, for bringing Scripture to life.

108 PAGES • 8½"x 11"

DOWNLOADABLE WITH OPTIONAL PAPERBACK

Praying by Number
Creative Prayer Lessons & Activities

- Two volumes, with 20 activities each.
- Fun and faith-filled ways to teach children and families how to talk to God.

76 PAGES PER VOLUME • 8½"x11"

DOWNLOADABLE WITH OPTIONAL PAPERBACK

by Anna L. Liechty & Phyllis Vos Wezeman

Experience the Saints — 4 Volumes
Activities for Multiple Intelligences

Eight activities per saint, each based on a different learning intelligence. Includes whole family and general classroom guides, with reproducible handouts.

- Vol. 1: Patrick, James, Hildegard of Bingen
- Vol. 2: Francis, Clare, Margaret of Scotland
- Vol. 3: Joan of Arc, Thomas Becket, Agnes
- Vol. 4: Peter, Catherine of Siena, Scholastica

200 PAGES PER VOLUME • 8½"x11" • DOWNLOADABLE

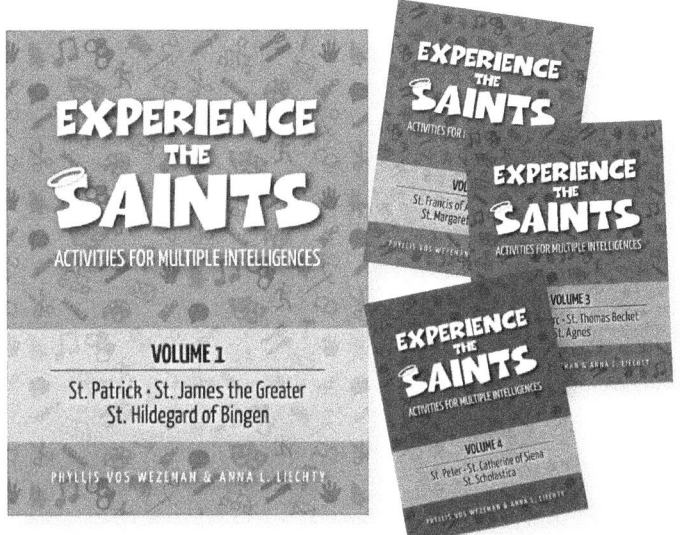

Seasons by Step: A Week-by-Week Thematic Approach

Use these creative approaches to explore a theme in-depth over the course of a season through Scripture. Each includes **talking points for children's messages, at-home family activities, artwork** for weekly symbols, and more.

Know Chocolate for Lent (Lent & Holy Week)
Uses the growing and manufacturing process of chocolate as a metaphor for the growth of faith and discipleship in the Christian life. Tools for parish-wide approach sold separately.
80 PAGES • DOWNLOADABLE

God's Family Tree (Lent & Holy Week)
Tracing the Story of Salvation

Tells the story of God's people as they struggle to find faith and hope for life through the symbols of trees found in Scripture. Includes optional Easter pageant and classroom activities.
114 PAGES • DOWNLOADABLE

In the Name of the Master (Advent/Christmas/Epiphany)
Sharing the Story of Christ

Uses a variation of the Advent wreath that uses fruits as symbols for the many names of God's Masterpiece, Jesus. Help your kids & families go deeper as they light their Advent candles each week.
37 PAGES • DOWNLOADABLE

http://pastoral.center/phyllis-vos-wezeman

 **The Pastoral Center** — *Pastoral ministers serving pastoral ministers*

http://pastoral.center • resources@pastoralcenter.com • Call us at 844-727-8672 (M-F 9am-5pm CT)

www.ingramcontent.com/pod-product-compliance
Lightning Source LLC
Chambersburg PA
CBHW080551170426
43195CB00016B/2756